BECAUSE
I LIVED IT

Surviving Widowhood

KATHRYN MONACO-DOUGLAS

D1523115

Inspira

Because I Lived It: Surviving Widowhood
First Edition 2025
Copyright © 2025 by Kathryn Monaco-Douglas

To order additional books:
www.amazon.com
www.widowednotalone.com

Visit www.widowednotalone.com

ISBN: 978-1-952943-46-1

E-book also available
ISBN: 978-1-952943-47-8

Editorial and Book Packaging: Inspira Literary Solutions, Gig Harbor, WA

Printed in the USA

I dedicate my book to Sister Anthony Therese.
Without her faith in me, none of what I accomplished
could have been possible.

. . . also, to Sister Kathleen McCarthy,
who helped me continue this ministry.

TABLE OF CONTENTS

TABLE OF CONTENTS

FOREWORD

by Alyson Lorenzo, a Recent Young Widow

One thing I am still working on is regaining the ability to write, like I once did. Nearly thirty minutes have transpired since sitting here, and I type, and I delete, and I type, and I delete.

Like many men and women grieving the loss of their spouse, the things that I used to be able to do with ease are now the most difficult. When Kathryn told me that it had been years since she could sit down with a book and read it (as opposed to listening to it), for the first time since losing Joe, I recognized myself in someone else and found my first connection.

It was about six months after my loss that I joined a grief support group. Due to COVID, groups were all virtual, which was a good thing for me, to be honest, as it reduced the pressure of actually having to move to go somewhere. Losing Joe had crippled me, and although the original thirteen members of that group are no longer quite as thick as thieves, it was through them that I made my subsequent connections, and it was then that the fog began to subside.

After eight sessions, when the group was over, our connections did not end. However, our Wednesday-night routine was
the only "new" routine to which I had committed, and without
it, I was, frankly, lost. This was when my relationship with Kathryn grew, and it was through our friendship that I learned of
her book. As an English teacher and "self-proclaimed" writer, I
offered to be her editor—if not for anything else, my commitment to her would certainly motivate me, right?

Well, it took longer than either of us would care to admit;
however, it was through her voice that I was able to regain
my own.

The truth is that the complexity surrounding what best
defines "better" or "okay" makes it difficult to feel and say that
I am. The language surrounding grief is so imprecise that there
is a massive gap in understanding between those who know
and those who don't know . . . yet. What I personally find
disturbing, for lack of a better word, is the lack of attention
grief receives. Ironically, we will all be here one day, and it's the
lack of conversation—the lack of acceptance for sadness—that
enhances the isolation and detachment we feel.

This loneliness can be all-consuming, and this hole in my
heart is permanent; this I know to be true. However, the only
companionship to be found within the isolation of this new
reality is from those who have also been kicked into it.

There's no going back. We are here. There are others like us.
Find them.

Our stories are timeless. Kathryn's story is timeless, and as
a newish member of the club, I can say with certainty that her

story does not hide behind the discomfort people feel when they talk about difficult things, and it does not sugarcoat the trauma of our tragedies. Just as our love is without end, so is our pain; in a world that operates by a clock, what do we do when ours stops?

If we look around a bit, the fog may dissipate for a moment, just at the right time, when someone else is trying to see through it, too.

Keep your eyes open and read the book.

Alyson Lorenzo
New York, New York
September 2024

PREFACE

At forty-two years old and with no warning, I was suddenly a widow raising my three children as a solo parent while grieving the sudden passing of my husband Larry.

As young as that may sound, I have met many widows younger than myself. This book shares some of their stories as well as my story, and how I survived it.

In 2023, the average age for a woman to be widowed was fifty-nine years old.[1] I found that age to be a shocking statistic. There are many different resources that I share in this book that I wish I had during my darkest times.

I never thought I would survive. I never thought I could ever find happiness again in this lifetime.

I would never have imagined that I would remarry a widower five years after my husband's passing.

One year after I remarried and six years after Larry passed, I began to immerse myself in the mission to help other young widows and widowers like Scott and me. We were both so

---

1. Balasek, Kathy. "Widows Are Younger Than You Think." Rethinking 65.com. https://rethinking65.com/2022/09/07/widows-are-younger-than -you-think/. Accessed September 10, 2024.

frustrated with the lack of support that I knew I wanted to go back to help others with their losses.

I felt then and still believe now that there aren't enough in-person resources for young widows and widowers. When I was going through my initial waves of grief, it shocked me that people were making the most ignorant and hurtful statements to me at a time when I needed them the most. Death isn't new . . . yet, how is it that after millennia of human history and experience, there isn't more awareness and understanding of how to help someone with early loss and continued grief?

Why is our society so grief illiterate, as grief specialist David Kessler states?

How is it that even some social workers and therapists don't know how to speak or treat a griever?

I have even witnessed some widows unintentionally hurting other widows because they think they know and understand everything about grief.

These thoughts often flooded my mind when I first started my journey. However, facilitating groups for close to two decades has taught me differently.

Grief is as individual as your fingerprint. The way in which one grieves encompasses so many factors, such as the individual's resiliency, past traumas, and coping mechanisms, as well as the relationship they had with the person who died and what took their life.

Grief is anything but linear; we think we are doing well and then we are suddenly back to having a bad day. The trauma of losing someone we love affects us all differently. However, spousal loss does have some common secondary losses that we all can share.

My journey in going back to help many over the years has left me with one last goal and that is to share it here, through this book, to reach more people with my story and what I have learned. No one can fix what happened, but I hope that my book will help you with how to help yourself.

Learning to Live with Loss

I learned one thing very quickly and that was that no one was going to save me but me. I needed to start by first opening my mind to different perspectives and, coming out of a married mindset, to learn how to step out of the comfort zone of a life I could never get back. I learned from many of the members of my group that many people marry their childhood sweethearts or someone they have spent almost a lifetime with, which makes moving forward all the more challenging.

When we lose our partners, we lose part of who we are. When I lost my Larry, I lost myself and was forever changed. I came back from the darkness of the depth of pain and suffering and with my return, my perspective on life changed and how I chose to live it.

Even if a couple never officially married, the loss of identity and purpose is still felt by the remaining partner, and I also refer to them as a "widow/widower" in this book. Unfortunately, society has not given fiancées, partners, boyfriends/girlfriends, etc. a respectful "title" after loss, which only makes them feel even more isolated and disconnected. Though couples may have lived together for years, the remaining partners can find themselves homeless, because the families take over. The unmarried are not entitled to Social Security benefits. This is called "disenfranchised grief," when someone doesn't feel they fit in in society after their loss—a grave injustice to those who are suffering. I have always included them in my groups.

Getting through grief is a lot of work and is exhausting. Many families, instead of becoming closer, are torn apart by their grief because we all express sadness and pain in different ways. Family members fight over the deceased assets. Siblings stop speaking. Childhood friendships end. In-laws point fingers. I have come to feel that no story shocks me any more of the cruelty that grief exhibits.

They say when one person dies, five people are affected deeply; my members say it's more like twenty. I recently received a call from an eighty-year-old woman who lost her mom in a tragic accident when she was a child. She said she is struggling now with that trauma because her whole life she avoided it— and now that she is elderly, and her life has slowed down, the tragedy is all she can think about and she needs help. I gave her the name of a therapist because too many years had passed for her to fit in any kind of conventional grief group.

This to me was a sad example of what can happen in the grief process, because she thought she had escaped it her whole life by staying busy. Is staying busy helpful? For some, it's a coping mechanism. It may feel helpful at the time, however, in the long term what happens to us? PTSD (post-traumatic stress disorder) flashbacks can remain for years depending on the complexities of your grief, and there is no medication at this time that can erase this.

I became obsessed with reading anything related to near-death experiences and people who claimed to have caught a glimpse of Heaven. I learned that people who died and came back shared experiences that totally changed them. They became more altruistic, and their perspective of life was forever altered. Similarly, when we lose our partners, we lose part of who we are. When I lost Larry, I lost myself and was forever changed. I came back from the darkness of the depth of pain and suffering, and with my return, my perspective on life changed, and on how I chose to live it.

Some coping tools that have helped many are found through trauma therapy. It's sad to say, but many people fight therapy, due to fear or a stigma. Or, they may have had a terrible experience and have chosen to not give anyone else a chance. I had experienced this as well. I have witnessed many members healing with the help of a good therapist. It's like we must kiss a lot of frogs before we find the right one.

At my husband's wake, my younger sister, Lisa, took me aside and said to me, "In a hundred years we will all be dead!" Even if it sounds morbid, that statement alone was enough to make me change the way I saw life and how I moved forward.

In one of my earlier groups, helping widows and widowers back in 2007, I received a compliment in the group from a man named Phil. He had tried five groups before finding mine and one night, when leaving the building, he said to me," You know why you're so good at this?' I just stared at him; I honestly didn't know what he was going to say. I think he thought I would instantly know, but I didn't. He said, "Because you lived it!"

I hope this book helps inspire you just as my groups have helped many over the years and help you learn that there is always hope.

CHAPTER 1

No More Goals

On a gray day in January of 2000, I lost my Larry. With that, I lost the love of my life and the life I cherished for twenty-three years.

"Why?" is such a simple word—a simple, short, one-syllable question that quickly becomes a complicated, burdensome interrogation about reality.

"Why would God take away a good man and an amazing father?" I remember asking these questions over and over on the night of Larry's death. I wasn't biblically knowledgeable, and no one consoling me was prepared to give me an answer.

People spoke in platitudes: "God has a plan." I'm sorry, was medical negligence part of the plan? That did not sit well with me. Are accidents part of God's divine plan?

"He is in a good place." Is being in Heaven better than being with me and his children, whom he loved dearly? I wanted to know for sure. I wanted to know where he was, how he was, what he was feeling, and where his soul was. How could Larry be happy in Heaven without us? We were everything to him, and he was everything to us.

Where in the Bible does it say such things? Where were these people getting these ideas? If this was "meant to be," it was because of a doctor's negligence, and what the hell could that possibly mean?

My Larry

It's normal to question your faith during loss. Many people often do. It was death alone that made me realize I was not in control of my life. Due to the weakened state of my faith at that time, I did not question *how* God allowed this to happen as much as I questioned *why*.

Nothing more tragic or devastating had ever happened to me and my children and the one person we needed desperately to speak to was the one person we didn't have. He was our go-to person.

A Surprising Conversation

Two weeks before my Larry died, he called me from work, something he always did. However, this call was different. He said to me, "I feel like I have no more goals."

I had no idea what he was talking about, and it annoyed me. I told him he was being ridiculous, and I hung up the phone.

When he arrived later that evening, he was eager to talk. "I need to speak with you, and I need you to sit down and listen to what I have to say." His face was still pink from the cold and the front door had barely closed behind him. I was standing in our kitchen, cooking dinner, when he made me put the spatula down. He took me by the hand and led me to our den, where we sat on the couch. He held both my hands.

"Don't take your eyes off mine. This is serious, and I need you to hear what I am about to say." He had the most beautiful blue eyes. "Goals," he said, "I feel like I have no more goals."

I gestured to pull my hands away and said, "Oh, no not this again?" but he wouldn't let me go.

"Hear me out." There was an unfamiliar urgency in his voice. "I feel that our business is exactly where I want it to be, our children are all so amazing; they are growing up so well and getting along so nicely. You and I are exactly where we need to be."

He was right. Our marriage had had its fair share of ups and downs over the years, but we had been on the right path for a while at that point. Our love and respect for each other was stronger than it had ever been. No one is perfect and relationships grow through the conflicts they withstand. We were two imperfect people who never gave up on each other and what felt like a very sudden and new discovery on his part caused me to feel confused and to be honest, disturbed.

"I don't understand," I said. "Don't you see how much we have ahead of us? The kids will graduate, get married, and then we'll have grandchildren someday. I'm confused; where is this coming from?"

"I am not asking you to agree with me," he said, cutting me off. "I'm just telling you how I feel, and I'm asking you to hear me and focus on what I'm telling you."

"Okay," I said, and I kissed him. I got up from the couch, pushed the whole conversation out of my mind, and walked back to the kitchen to finish cooking dinner.

On the evening that Larry passed away, my house was packed. I mean packed, with wall-to-wall people. My sisters and my mother must have called every family member we had. Our friends, our kids' friends, and their parents all came over. It was a circus, but it was also comforting to be surrounded by so many people who shared the same overwhelming feeling of shock.

I remember feeling like a zombie, barely able to move by myself. My mother was pushing me toward the front door to see Lucy, a woman from my neighborhood, and her daughter. Rosie was a thin, petite woman of forty or so, with a brunette pixie haircut and big, soft, brown eyes. She was sweet yet timid in her body language, and I think I may have met her only once before. She was a Eucharistic minister at my church. She walked right up to me, holding in her hands a small metal bowl filled with tiny medals the size of a coin.

Raising a medal to my face she said, "God has a goal for Larry."

"Wait! What?" I stared at her and took a deep breath. "Can you say that again?" I was shocked by her words.

She repeated, "God has a goal for Larry." The hair on the back of my neck stood at full attention, extending from the goosebumps that covered my entire body. I felt like I was watching a movie. It was a flashback from two weeks prior when I was sitting in the den with Larry, his hands firmly holding mine, and I listened to him go on and on about the feelings he had about having no more goals.

I hugged Rosie and wept in her arms. "Is that why God took my Larry?" I said between tears. "Is that why? Because God had a goal for him?" She looked at me like a deer in headlights. I felt her love for me in the pain I was feeling.

I had not told anyone about my conversation with Larry that evening. Now it was much less of a conversation than a premonition. How could he have known? He was so serious, so insistent that I listen to him and understand exactly how he felt.

I needed to process what had just happened and I needed to process it alone. Moving in what felt like slow motion, I managed to make it to our den, where I lay down on the floor and wept, clasping the tiny medal in my hand. I wore that medal around my neck all the time. Today it hangs on a crucifix next to the nightstand beside my bed. The crucifix was what I was handed when they closed the casket. The medal represents to me the goal that Larry has with God—a goal I knew nothing about.

Many years later, a therapist helped me realize that God had given Larry the insight to know his life here on Earth was complete. She asked me to describe Larry to her, and as I did I felt so strongly his presence in the room and the goosebumps on my arms were proof of what I was thinking. I didn't want her to think I was crazy, so I didn't tell her. But, just as I finished describing him, on the very final syllable of my sentence, the lamp in the corner of her room shut off.

"Has that ever happened before?" I asked. When she said it had not, I confessed. "I know you're going to think I am crazy for saying this, but he is here. I could feel him as soon as you asked me to describe him." It would be just like my Larry, not wanting to miss hearing me bragging about him.

Without missing a beat, she said, "He probably is." She gestured for me to continue, never once making me feel uncomfortable or embarrassed for sharing those thoughts with her. I truly appreciated it that I had finally found a good therapist to help me work through my trauma.

My mother slept with me for three months after Larry died. During that first week, there was one night when I woke up to the feeling that there was a presence over my bed. I thought one of my children was next to my bed, but when I opened my eyes, no one was there. I turned to look at my mother, and to my surprise, she was awake. I lightly nudged her shoulder and whispered, "Go back to sleep."

In the morning, I asked her why she was awake in the middle of the night, and she said she woke up to the feeling that there was a presence over the bed. We had the same experience! Of course, I wondered if it was Larry's spirit coming back to say goodbye. If I knew Larry at all, he would be having a difficult time leaving us.

When my mother went back to Florida, my eleven-year-old daughter Danielle took her place in my bed. I would have let her stay with me forever, but my first therapist advised that this wasn't healthy for Danielle. I knew it was me who was clinging to my daughter, not the other way around. I did what I thought was right and I put Danielle back in her own bed.

I have known many widows who do this; I am not judging, just sharing. I must admit I was grateful to my therapist for giving me this advice. I realized it was selfish of me to have her sleep with me and not have her own independence.

Later, when I remarried—something I truly could have never imagined happening—I realized this had been for the best. My daughter would have resented giving up her sleeping arrangements for my new husband.

The undertaker who prepared Larry's body for his funeral gave me a quarter, which he said he found on Larry's body. This was strange because Larry was naked on his way to the shower when he died. I stared at the quarter, looking for answers, and I read, "In God We Trust." Maybe I was looking too hard, but in my despair, I needed something.

CHAPTER 2

Brooklyn Girl

In processing my grief over Larry's death, I learned that childhood traumas will emerge with more recent trauma. Our childhood affects who we are for the rest of our lives.

There is a popular expression where I come from: "You can take the girl out of Brooklyn, but you can't take Brooklyn out of the girl." The first question I'm asked when people hear me speak is, "What part of Brooklyn are you from?" In fact, my now-husband Scott's first impression of my accent was that I am a dead ringer for Marissa Tomei's character in the movie *My Cousin Vinny.*

I am every bit five feet tall, but boy, am I feisty! I was raised by an Italian-American Catholic family in Bensonhurst Brooklyn, where we rented the top floor of what was hardly a two-family home, sandwiched between two unrelated families, one occupying the attic above us, and the landlord occupying the floor below. My two sisters, mother, father, maternal grandmother, and I shared two bedrooms and one bathroom for the better part of ten years.

When I was seven and my sister Roseanne was nine, our parents threw us a dual Communion and Confirmation party, the first party I can recall as a child. Our space was limited, so the capacity to entertain was as well, which made it obvious when anyone arrived or left. Before the party ended, my father left to return borrowed food racks to the restaurant that catered our affair. His absence was noted. A few hours later, his absence became worrisome. When it was determined that his absence would be permanent, our family was changed forever. Later, we found out he had a girlfriend, and within weeks, my mother had a nervous breakdown.

I can remember the broken English, screaming from the panic-stricken voice of my Italian grandmother as she pleaded with a doctor from our house phone "to com-ah, to com-ah, please-ah, right away." My mom would not wake up. This was traumatic at seven years old—a flashback I vividly remember to this day.

After three days of watching milk pour from the sides of my mother's mouth—unresponsive to my grandmother's attempts to nurse her—my sisters and I were sent out, and out of my grandmother's desperation, the priest was called in. When we came home, my mom was awake, sitting beside her was Father Anastasia, a priest from our school. Her eyes were sealed shut for three whole days; it was as though she had to train them to open again, but when she finally did, the small glimmer I saw shining through told me that she could see even more clearly. Father Anastasia saved my mother. I don't know exactly what he said to her, but whatever it was, it enabled her to realize she had us and that we were important enough to live for. We jumped on her bed, and we laughed, we cried, and it was probably the most memorable time of my childhood. I was so happy to feel my mother's love again.

Learning to Cope

Our widowed grandmother quit her job to take care of us so that my stay-at-home mother could now work full-time. That first year she worked nights, and when we arrived home from school, my grandmother would be the only one there. It felt as though we had been orphaned, essentially losing both of our parents at the same time. My grandmother became a second mother to us. However, as much as we loved her, no one replaces your real parents.

A year later we were forced to move to a new location. This was another loss for us all, the landlord was giving our apartment to her daughter. We lost everything we knew, and as kids, we couldn't communicate or comprehend much of what was going on.

This is when I started praying. I can remember crying myself to sleep frequently, begging God to bring my father back. I cried, I questioned, I bargained, and I begged, but he never came. I felt abandoned, not just by my father and mother, but by God. I blamed my father's actions for all our misfortune. It was because of him, I thought that even God stopped caring about all of us.

In 1970, I graduated from the eighth grade, and to celebrate, my friends and I went to a local restaurant named Fluffy's

Pancake House. I had once overheard that my father worked there, so when my grandmother allowed me to go with my friends that day, it was because I intentionally left out where we were going.

The restaurant had an open kitchen, and from where we were sitting, I could clearly see the row of cooks—an assembly line of white jackets and tall chef hats, chopping and dicing and mixing and grilling. I thought I could see him through the line of coats, arranging things behind them. I told my friends, and they encouraged me to say hello. Though I was incredibly nervous after not seeing him for five years, I picked myself up from the table, adjusted my skirt, and walked toward the kitchen.

I snuck in through the swinging doors that separate the hustle of the kitchen from the much less boisterous ambiance of the dining room. I saw him bending down, loading a dishwasher, and I nervously tapped his shoulder. I didn't want to startle him but to no avail—he stood up, stared at me, and he paused. I remember questioning, *Does he know who I am?* Five years can do a lot to a young girl's appearance.

I was frozen in fear; I could not, and I did not, say a word. Before I knew what happened next, he was sobbing. He grabbed me all in one swift movement and held me to him. Over and over, through tears and what I can only now assume was tremendous guilt, he hugged me, kissed my cheek, and told me he loved me. At that moment, I became more aware of myself than I ever had been before, realizing just how much his absence pained me, and how much I still wanted him to come home. I knew that I loved him and that wasn't going to change, but it was only when I saw him that I truly recognized how much I missed him. I missed the comfort of my father's arms and the safety of his presence; I missed the significance of what my father should have been, and I was ashamed. I was ashamed to love someone whose love for us was questionable—every missed birthday, holiday, gathering, or event was followed up with the same question: "Where's daddy?"

I was ashamed that I missed and loved so much the man who made my mother have a breakdown and broke her heart. I felt that I was harboring a secret from my mother not to hurt her more.

Moving Forward

Do we ever get over past pains from our childhood, or do those scars make us who we are to this present day? A child should never harbor love or keep it a secret for fear of how it may affect someone else. This is often a problem that challenges children of divorce, and it's something parents should be aware of. I am grateful that my mother never verbally trashed my father, but she did say that one day, we would see for ourselves, and she was right.

When I was going through puberty and becoming sassy, I threatened to leave my mother to go live with my father. She said, "Go right ahead and see if he wants you!" Those words remained with me for years. My father didn't want me, and sadly I knew it. It wasn't just that he left my mother that hurt so much, but the feeling that we, his own flesh and blood were forgotten.

It would be close to a decade before I saw him again. I felt that he came in and out of our lives like breadcrumbs, always a quick visit here and there, as if it were done by obligation and not by love.

At seventeen years old, my family left the streets of Brooklyn for the quaint suburbs of Long Island. My sisters and I were faced with another huge adjustment. We were street smart in Brooklyn; you had to be.

But on Long Island, there were more trees than streets, and when you come from the streets, Long Island is the country. Little did we know that my father had a thing for the country too.

My sisters and me—Lisa on left; Roseanne on right

CHAPTER 3

No One Is Coming to Save You

When we moved to Long Island, my mother found a program called Boces that taught high schoolers a trade. My mother told me that I wasn't college material. I always loved art, but she discouraged me that artists couldn't make a good living. I also liked cutting hair. I cut my neighbor's hair and my uncles', and I guess I was good because they always came back.

However, the cosmetology course was full, and the only opening was in Medical Assisting.

I never thought I would like it, but I ended up loving it. I had the highest grade in my class, which prompted a recommendation to a local hospital. At eighteen years old, I was working as an EKG technician and later trained in EEGs and Respiratory. I really found something I liked and excelled at.

At twenty-one years old, I was with Larry, who was my boyfriend at the time. Larry caught hepatitis and had to go to the hospital. The hospital was in Smithtown, Long Island, where I was working. I was sitting on the bed visiting Larry when he received a call from one of my family members. I'll never forget the look on his face when Larry uttered the words, "Your father has been shot." I don't think he ever forgot the look on mine.

My father was admitted to the intensive care unit at Brunswick Hospital in Amityville. After all those years of his abandonment, I couldn't help but fear and question whether I had ever told him I loved him.

He had been shot in the face. The bullet entered through his right cheek and exited out of his left. His tongue was blown apart, and many of his teeth were crushed. I tried to have him transferred to the hospital where I worked, but moving him was too high of a risk. I wanted to take care of him. Instead, I stayed with a friend who lived in the area.

W. Babylon Man Charged With Attempted Murder

Hauppauge—A man who police say shot another man in a dispute over a woman was being held in lieu of $50,000 bail on an attempted murder charge.

Police said that the suspect, Saverio (Frank) Urcuiolio, shot Joseph Alletto early Friday morning. Alletto was in stable condition last night at Brunswick Memorial Hospital in Amityville.

Officers said that the shooting occurred after Alletto returned from a date with Gladys Franco at about 3 AM. Urcuiolio, who had parked his car outside the woman's house at 633 Sixth St., West Babylon, shot Alletto in the face with a .38-cal. revolver, telling him "I hope you had fun with my girlfriend," police said.

Urcuiolio, 51, of 1101 12th St., West Babylon, fled, and Ms. Franco called police. Alletto, 45, was rushed to the hospital. Police said that they have been unable to determine the victim's home address.

Shortly after the shooting, two New York City Port Authority policemen, Al Lopez and Vincent Ortiz, who had finished work at midnight, stopped at the Say-When Bar on Route 109.

Ortez said he heard a man on the pay phone outside say "I just shot a guy. He was with my girlfriend. I love her." Police say that Ortiz arrested the man, identified as Urcuiolio. The suspect allegedly was carrying a .38-cal. revolver in his pocket.

Urcuiolio was arraigned in First District Court. A hearing was set for Wednesday.

He could not speak,   *Newspaper article about the shooting*
but he would watch me
taking care of him daily. On one particular day, while wiping drool from his face, I noticed tears that would need to be wiped away as well.

16

I knew at that moment he recognized that he did not deserve this loving treatment from me, the daughter he had abandoned for so many years. Honestly, he didn't.

My relationship with my father changed after that; he tried his best to be in my life, and I tried my best to let him. I do believe that we never know what someone is going through, making them act the way they do. My husband Larry had this expression: "The blood pulls."

No matter what my father did or did not do he was still my father, and I would forgive him. Larry somehow knew.

Managing Expectations

I do believe that my childhood helped me to develop a different type of relationship regarding expectations. I finally understood my father's limitations and how to manage my expectations.

It was up to me to learn and truly understand that people are only capable of what they are, not what we want them to be.

I grew up with the feelings of unworthiness, which come when a parent abandons you. Maybe if I was a better child he would have stayed? Or maybe, if I had been the son he always wanted? Children have these types of thoughts. I just never shared mine.

Our childhood affects the rest of our lives in ways we sometimes do not realize. I learned that letting go and being a victim is a choice; holding on to pain can only limit growth. The trauma wasn't my fault, but the healing was my responsibility. If we continue to drown in the pain of the past or continue to hold onto anger toward others who caused us pain, we unknowingly invite them to join us in the future—and rob that as well.

When I was a child, I never went to therapy. At that time, there were more stigmas surrounding therapy than there are now. Those who required therapy were often assumed to be disturbed. As an older adult, I went into therapy to help me with the unworthy beliefs I carried for many years. After Larry's death, feelings of abandonment flooded me again and I recognized the need for therapy.

I thought my father's abandonment was the worst thing that I could have ever lived through. That was an assumption.

Grieving Loss and Change

On the first night of Larry's wake, a woman came to speak with me. She had lost her only daughter at eighteen in a car accident. She told me to prepare myself for the firsts.

"Firsts?" I thought I had no idea what she was talking about.

"First birthday, first anniversary, first Father's Day, first Thanksgiving, first Christmas, and the first New Year," she explained to me, leaving me in a state of complete shock.

Looking back now, the fact that she put her feelings aside to give me this advice was an incredible act of kindness, and I will be forever grateful. This one simple act of kindness bestowed upon me on the day of Larry's wake taught me what it felt like to be on the receiving end of a kind gesture in the darkest of times. It's incredible how one simple act can be so impactful

Our Family

for someone who lived it. I make it a point to pay it forward whenever I can.

I realized the importance of speaking with my children prior to their father's funeral. This would be the first funeral they had ever attended, and I worried about their reactions. I told my boys that I was relying on them to avoid any outbursts as I feared how it would affect their little sister. I didn't want her to be more traumatized than she already was.

I made a point to tell each of them that this was not "goodbye" but rather "so-long." At the cemetery, as I placed a rose atop Larry's coffin, my eighteen-year-old son Michael wrapped his arms around me from behind and whispered into my ear,

"So long, so long, so long," repeatedly as we walked out of the chapel, holding me in the tightest bear hug the whole way out.

◇◇◇

In the early days after losing Larry, on the occasions that we sat at our table with bags of fast food, my two sons would argue about who would take their father's place at the dinner table. I sat in Larry's chair and told them that neither of them was to feel like the "new man of the house."

It wasn't until later, however, that I learned of Michael's experience during the week of Larry's wake. Everyone felt the need to pull my son aside because he was the eldest and tell him that he was, in fact, the man of the house now. For a grieving eighteen-year-old boy, I can't even imagine the pressure he felt.

It caused fights between his siblings as they needed a brother, not a boss. It caused conflicts in our family dynamic. I did not want Michael to take on this role and truthfully neither did he, nor should he have to. I recently was told by one of my members that her five-year-old son was told the same.

This is one reason I believe education in grief is so important. People believe they are helping. I do believe they mean well, but they are indeed contributing to more pain.

Therapy Failure #1

I sought out a young male therapist to work with Michael. I thought he would relate to a young man. He was verbalizing how much he couldn't handle what we were dealing with. My children were incredibly close with their dad. I thought this would be a good connection for my son.

Michael walked into the doctor's office, looked around, and after five minutes he asked the therapist how long he had been separated from his wife. The therapist was surprised by his question and asked how Michael knew he and his wife had separated. "I noticed your pictures around your office, and they are only of you and your son. So, am I right?"

"Actually, my wife and I are separated," replied the therapist.

"So when did you lose your dad?" Michael asked.

"I never lost my dad."

My son was displeased, to say the least. "You can't keep your marriage together and you never lost your father. How the hell are you going to help me?"

To my surprise, Michael stepped into the waiting room and said "Mom, keep your money! This guy can't figure out his own life. He can't help me!"

I tried to convince my son that this therapist was trained in matters of grief, but deep in my heart I knew Michael was right. How does one understand the depth of this pain of grief from a book?

Not long after the therapist incident, a speaker for the DARE program spoke about drug abuse at the high school. The speaker—a police officer—happened to mention that he had lost his dad. Michael's girlfriend was in the auditorium and asked the officer if he would speak to her boyfriend who recently was struggling. That kind man, Pauly, spent hours on the phone helping my son.

Because he had experienced it firsthand, another hero saved the day.

Therapy Failure #2

In the early stages of my grief, I met with only one therapist, a woman in her sixties, whom I went to see at night after work. During my visit, she closed her eyes while I spoke, but I said nothing.

During our next visit, she did it again, only this time I could not hold back. "Are you falling asleep?" I was feeling invisible.

"I'm listening," she responded, "with my eyes closed."

"Okay," I said calmly, but inside, I was hurt. I was so angry and frustrated. I knew I was never going back. There was no way I was going to pay for this kind of therapy.

It made me think back to a time when my youngest wanted to read to me, and I was so tired that I would lay in bed and assure her that Mommy was listening with her eyes closed. I'll admit from time to time, I tried to sneak in a little nap.

Who could possibly do that to someone in therapy? I was paying this woman to listen to me and to help me with my grief. My grief was so intense I didn't know which end was up, and here she was with her eyes closed, pretending to listen. Maybe she wasn't actually sleeping, but I was actually insulted.

◇◇◇

We provide our members with a list of therapists' names, who specialize in grief. There is support for grief, and no one should have to go through this without it.

Lynn, one of my most recent members, texted me because her therapist told her to avoid speaking about her husband so much, and she didn't know how she felt about it. I told her she could not be told to stop speaking about him, and she should not do anything she didn't want to do. This is all part of her trauma and it's why she was seeing this therapist to begin with!

One year later, it was me who helped her through one-on-one coaching. She felt that I understood her better *because I have lived it.*

Another member was told by her therapist to forget about all the dates, the birthdays, the anniversaries, and whatever else reminded her of him. How? This is an impossible challenge you will not win. Spend your energy elsewhere.

I read in the book *Continuing Bonds* by Dennis Klass, Phyllis R. Silverman, and Steen L. Nickman, that a hundred years ago that was how they handled grief—by detaching and not speaking of their loss. I have never stopped speaking about Larry. I thought about him all the time; how could I possibly not speak of him? I truly become infuriated by trained professionals who are ignorant and give poor advice to those who are grieving.

We are not going to "get over them." There is nothing to get over. There is no timeline to grief, and no one should make you feel that there is.

CHAPTER 4

The Effects of Grief

My now-husband Scott was also unexpectedly widowed. He and his first wife, Sally, married on the third day of August in 1986. She passed one day short of their thirteenth anniversary from a surgery gone wrong.

It was discovered, upon returning from a routine gynecological visit, that Sally had a very rare form of cancer. Whilst lying flat on the table, the physician noticed a bulge in her abdomen. It only took one CT scan to determine that the bulge was, in fact, a desmoid tumor, and though it was contained, it was cancerous and would need to be extracted.

They operated right away. With three young children at home, all under the age of ten, there was no time to waste, but that did not prevent Scott from finding the most capable surgeon to perform her surgery. He was a specialist in his field and operated out of the top cancer hospital in Manhattan. He performed his surgery, and his residents closed her up.

Everything appeared to be falling right into place.

With the surgery complete, Scott and Sally could go home and be with their children, heal, and move forward from what could have been a nightmare.

But the nightmare ensued. Sally's post-operative recovery was not going as planned; for an entire week she complained that something did not feel right, yet her concerns were disregarded by the nurses and doctors to whom she aired them. They lessened the dosage of pain medication she was prescribed, as they assumed her symptoms were not in connection to them. Only one week later, it was determined she would require another emergency surgery. A blood clot had formed where the surgery had been performed, effectively compromising her intestines. She would return home, but would be outfitted with a feeding tube and a colostomy bag to replace her gangrenous intestines.

Scott went into survival mode. He investigated nannies to help care for his three young children, and he became the primary caregiver for his wife. Due to the nature of Sally's surgeries, they quickly determined they had been the victims of medical negligence and went forward with filing a suit against the hospital.

Two years later, Sally underwent another surgery, this time in Pittsburg. It took twenty-five hours to replace her intestines, but it only took a few hours in recovery for a fungus to develop and cause a stroke, effectively taking her life at the ripe age of forty-four.

As followers of the Jewish faith, it is tradition to bury the departed the day after their final breath, but Scott asked Sally's mother to wait one day so as not to bury her on the anniversary of the day they promised each other forever. She agreed, and as he packed up everything from their apartment in Pittsburg, his mind was overwrought with the detail required for setting up funeral arrangements, speaking with family and friends, and above all, how to tell his three

Scott and Sally

young children that their mother had died. He refused to tell them over the phone, so it was on the actual day of her funeral that they learned of the tragedy.

Brett, their eldest son, was angry with Scott—he wanted to say goodbye.

Children and Grief

Scott and Sally's youngest daughter, Jordana, was two when Sally became ill and four when she died. She did not speak after Sally's death. The trauma was too much for her. To get her to speak again, she went to a therapist who used puppet therapy—a form of play therapy that involves the use of puppets by mental health professionals for diagnostic and therapeutic purposes. After five and a half weeks, Jordana found her voice again. Their oldest son, Brett, was eleven, he was angry, and his outbursts and temper tantrums became incredibly difficult to contend with. He also went to therapy, but it didn't help.

Their middle boy, Zachary, was six, and he appeared to be doing better than the other two, but appearances can be deceiving, and though Zach managed his grief reasonably well, he was far from unscathed. Zach's inability to share his grief reminded me of my own detachment from my dad leaving. I knew the mentality: if we don't speak about it, it's like it really didn't happen.

Like adults, children all grieve differently. In my opinion, from working with so many widows and widowers, I see that many children have delayed grief.

In a survey I conducted with members of my group, out of ninety-eight people, 71 percent stated that their children had delayed grief. Fifteen percent said their children had shown no signs of grief. In this brief study, I didn't ask how long ago their loss was, which may indicate that they haven't experienced their grief yet.

My mom lost her dad when she was eighteen and she always told us the story of how it wasn't until she woke up the morning of her nineteenth birthday that she realized her dad was dead. I didn't understand how it took her a year. I now understand that she was experiencing delayed grief.

My best friend Ella told me she did the exact same thing a year after the death of her dad.

There is inevitable stored trauma associated with loss, and it should never be ignored. Many children suppress their emotions during grief, which can create physical ailments—I have heard endless stories of children who have developed physical symptoms that range from headaches to stomachaches to eating disorders and attempted suicides. If children are willing to go to therapy, establishing a relationship with a therapist could be their lifeline. They won't necessarily need to go weekly, but having and maintaining the connection has proven to be incredibly helpful. I will write more about children's grief in future chapters.

I saw an interview that Anderson Cooper did for *60 Minutes* on CBS in January of 2023 with Prince Harry of England. He was twelve years old when his mother, Princess Diana, was killed. He refused to speak to anyone about it. He shared that he didn't shed a tear. He remembered greeting mourners the day before his mom's funeral and that all the people who were coming were sobbing, yet he and his brother couldn't. Admirers of his mom were handing them flowers with wet hands from their tears, and he and his brother, William, were placing them with the rest in a pile. Deep grief was felt by many around the world, but her own sons were numb to it.

After the service, as her coffin was lowered into the ground, Harry stated he cried only that once and he never cried after that. He refused to believe she was dead, for many, many years.

This is a true example of delayed grief. He said, and I am paraphrasing, that in his twenties he went into the military where he found real purpose. He was angry at the British Press because he felt they were responsible for her death, and he started abusing alcohol and drugs. I understood what he was sharing. The private secretary refused to show him the rest of the graphic photos the accident that took her life, knowing we can't erase what we see. In retrospect, Prince Harry said, he was glad they held them back.

However, he did feel he needed to make it real. He went back to the scene of the accident, where his mom was killed. Even at the time of the interview, he sounded like he was really struggling with the emotions never released. He ended up seeking heavy therapy to deal with the trauma, anger, frustration, and shame that were still affecting him from so many years ago. He felt shame because he couldn't cry.

The first mistake would be to assume children are not affected by loss just because you're not seeing it. If your child broke his leg, you wouldn't ignore it. We can't ignore their broken hearts. And what about *your* pain?

Your children know you better than anyone; we only think we are hiding our pain from them, and while some children will do everything they can to try and make you feel better, others, like my teens, will find anywhere else to be besides being home.

We need to have communication with our children about our grief, and there are healthy ways to share it so that we can manage life with it and live through it together.

Younger children, like Scott's, did not even know how to articulate what they were feeling. It wasn't until their teens that two of the three were triggered by the ending of a relationship. We never know what will cause the grief to be activated, it could be the loss of a pet, moving from a home, a grandparent passing away, or something that occurs at school.

I recently saw the movie *Elvis*, and in the movie, it was revealed that Elvis was a twin; however, his twin brother died at birth and his mother never got over it. It seemed that her coping mechanism was alcohol. She drank until she killed herself.

Elvis, distraught over her death, subsequently welcomed drugs and alcohol into his life. I see these life stories and I can't help but wonder if anyone else is recognizing what I do.

I recognize that, like Elvis, the coping mechanism they choose is drugs or alcohol instead of walking in nature, seeking a therapist, finding a support group, or journaling. I believe most people don't seek a healthy choice because they may not believe one exists. If this describes your family's situation, I encourage you to keep watch over your kids and their behavior, especially if they are not acting appropriately for their loss.

I strongly believe in the power of a positive connection with a professional for your child. You can interview different therapists and evaluate who you think will have the best connection first. I believe it's worth your time because, like me, you may have only one opportunity for your child to meet this therapist, so you want it to be the right person. I would ask the therapist what training they have in helping children with grief. Regardless of how it is manifested, this relationship is ever so important in your child's ability to heal.

I also believe it's okay to show feelings in front of your children, like tears. How else will they learn that showing your feelings is normal? I am not speaking of an all-out panic attack but showing your sadness is okay. We need to release pain and not suppress it and we need them to feel free to do the same. I had a woman on my Instagram who shared that she cries in her closet so her children won't witness her sadness. She felt she needed to protect them.

There is nothing shameful about feeling sad when someone we love dies. Healthy grief is, after all, a demonstration of our love for them, and our feelings of loss that they are no longer with us.

Teens are especially difficult at articulating their grief to anyone. Some of my members have given their children notebooks to journal as an alternative. This is an excellent way, for them to express their feelings.

Our Words Have Power

I have learned that the words we say to our children impact them. I met a man named Rex at a wake who shared something I thought was profound.

He said when he was eight years old, and his brother was an infant, his dad passed away. He looked up at his mom and said, "What are we going to do now?"

His mom, weeping, said, "I have no idea!"

He expressed to me that his mother's words were frightening to him and that, at that moment in time, he felt the pressure to help her whenever he could. He felt his childhood was robbed from him. He did his chores, did well in school, and worked at an early age, always feeling like he had to replace his dad in some way.

He was very interested in speaking with me because he had heard about the work I do and wanted to share his perspective. I really appreciated his honesty and boldness to come forward. I left the conversation wondering if I ever used those words with my own children.

I'm almost certain that I made my children believe we could get through it together. We all knew what Daddy would want from us.

Younger children take whatever you say literally. Never say Mommy or Daddy went to sleep instead of saying they died. They will be petrified to go to sleep. One of my members, as a child was told Grandma went to Florida when she died, and she was petrified to go to Florida. Our words matter and we want to be honest so they know they can trust us.

Don't Trust the Wolf in Sheep's Clothing

When Scott held *shiva*[2] for Sally at their home, people from everywhere came over to express their condolences. One woman, recently divorced, made an advance toward Scott. His disgust at this implication was something that has never truly left him.

It is not as uncommon to be the target for "single" men and women as most people would think; even cheating married men and women who are unhappy in their marriage may try to take advantage of someone who is vulnerable. This is a common story I have heard throughout my years of leading support

---

2. In Judaism, *shiva* is the seven-day mourning period for the immediate family of the deceased. Its primary purpose is to create an environment of comfort and community for mourners, helping guide friends and family members through the loss of their loved one. Throughout the weeklong shiva period, mourners come together in one family's home to offer their condolences and support.

groups. I have heard from many men who talk about the "single neighbor with a tray of food." This approach may be a red flag. I'm not saying some of these relationships haven't worked out because a few have; however, more have not.

Don't be naïve. Dating a man who says he is separated but lives in the same house as his estranged wife "for financial reasons," is too risky. You have been through so much; it's not worth the hurt that will inevitably happen in a situation like this.

You are worthy of more.

Many grievers, and certainly in the beginning stages of grief, are not seeing or hearing things clearly.

The prefrontal cortex of our brain is hijacked by grief, the part of our brain that is responsible for executive function, like concentration, focus, and decision-making. I believe this is why many people don't see the red flags. There is a fog that seems to linger around our thought process.

We certainly cannot decipher what a person's intentions are by a tray of food. I can't help but think that there is a strategy at play in situations where a man or woman suggests, "If you need to talk, I'm here for you." Just be careful. There are people out there who seek to take advantage, and when given the smallest opportunity, they will. If someone honestly wants to help, they will recommend a bereavement group or a therapist. If they are sincere, they will wait until you are mentally in a better place. Many people who get into a relationship to avoid their pain will fall back into heavy grief, guilt, and regret if it doesn't work out. Sometimes this happens years later, and they lose the opportunity to be in a support group.

I had a woman in one of my groups, Dawn, who dropped out after a few sessions. Six years later, she contacted me and wanted to repeat. She had remarried and was now divorced, and her new husband inherited quite a bit of her inheritance from her late husband. She shared with us that, after the divorce, he revealed that he had stalked her using information gleaned from her husband's obituary in the newspaper.

Figuring out who you are after you lose your spouse is so important. Getting into a relationship too soon and trusting this new person without doing a Google search on them (or other kind of background check) is not safe. Sometimes just looking up their Facebook or other social media profile can be very revealing. It's worth your time and even your money to see if they have any kind of criminal record.

One woman I met, Susan, was dating someone for three years only to find out after a physical altercation with her son that he was a registered sex offender. If the altercation hadn't happened, she would have never researched him. "I knew him from the neighborhood," she explained" Besides her son, Susan had a young daughter. I suggested to her that she let her daughter know the truth about him—and never to speak to him or get in the car with him, because now he was a familiar face.

I had another woman in one of my groups whose boyfriend was physically abusing her, and she was allowing it because she was afraid of being alone.

These women needed to do work on themselves to realize they were worthy of much more than what they were settling for. You know what real love feels like; you were married to it.

Don't panic and don't settle.

Many women and men, as I mentioned in the introduction, have married their high school sweethearts. We can't meet the right person if we spend time with the wrong one. I also believe that you sometimes find the right person when you aren't looking so hard, which is how I met Scott.

If you never want to meet anyone or date anyone again, that is okay too. In my group, plenty of people have been friends for years, enjoying picnics, bowling, restaurants, wineries, and cruises. The group camaraderie helps those not feel so alone. This is just another reason to contemplate joining a support group.

I, personally, also had to do a lot of self-work after my husband died. We develop our belief system from childhood, and it shadows over our adulthood. I unknowingly developed a lower self-image due to my dad's abandonment, believing I was not important enough for him to stay home. Since Larry was the bright light and the one who kept me out of my dysfunctional upbringing, I also believe, in retrospect, that I had a co-dependency on him. When he died, I was so incredibly lost.

I recently read two great books that I highly recommend in helping you with your self-esteem: *Self-Compassion: The Proven Power of Being Kind to Yourself*, by Kristin Neff, and *Honoring the Self: The Psychology of Confidence and Respect* by Nathaniel Branden. They are both available on Amazon in print, e-book, and audio versions.

Self-work is having self-compassion for your grief. What does that mean? You may feel you made some mistakes like in the raising of your children or in someone you dated. It could be you decided on something that you later are sorry for. We need to be less judgmental about ourselves. Some of our relationships are complex after loss because we are super sensitive and others are so unaware of our changes.

I like to say, "I am perfectly imperfect."

CHAPTER 5

Stepping Out of
The Comfort Zone

At forty-two years old, Scott found himself raising three children alone. Of course, he had help from the nannies he hired and fired and hired again—he fired a total of thirty-one nannies in five years. These women robbed his home, lied to him, and many would leave on a Friday, never to return. This would prove to be yet another form of abandonment for his children.

Scott was struggling with how to navigate fatherhood without Sally by his side. After some research, he joined a bereavement group for young widows and widowers at a local center in Commack, Long Island. This is where Scott and I met.

It was April of 2000, three and a half months after I lost Larry and eight months since Scott had lost Sally.

As I walked into a room, I saw twelve younger-looking people. Four men and eight women were sitting in a circle, with only one empty seat remaining.

I took the empty seat, which happened to be the seat right next to Scott. I looked at him with a forced, sad smile, and I remember the amazement I felt at the fact that all these people were just like me.

I was often late wherever I went, a habit I later made a conscious effort to break.

I noticed upon scanning the room that everyone wore jeans, for the most part; some wore sweatpants. Scott, however, caught my attention because he was wearing business clothes—dress pants and a white, neatly pressed button-down shirt adorned with a red tie. Every hair on his head was sprayed neatly into place, including what I remember thinking was a really out-dated Geraldo Rivera mustache. It wasn't until we were stand-ing that I realized how tall he was. Tall and lean at a cool six feet and two inches.

An attractive, blonde-haired woman named Felicia was our facilitator. She put herself together nicely, and I noticed she was sitting on her hands while speaking. Sometimes, I hate how observant I can be. As a visual person, I can recall information in such detail, like a photograph of a moment frozen in time, in my head.

Having a photographic memory can be an advantage at times, but after the loss, it was a nightmare.

The facilitator asked each person, "How exactly did you lose your spouse?"

She started our first meeting by asking each of us to provide the details of our losses, interjecting with remarks about how her loss was similar somehow. I remember thinking, *Wow! She too is in this horrible club no one wants to join.*

I remember feeling like I was in that Jack Nicholson movie based on the book *One Flew Over the Cuckoo's Nest*. My grief made me feel like I was going crazy, and connecting with a loony bin circa 1975 felt apropos.

As I was sitting in my circle, with Scott sitting next to me and each person sharing and triggering and detailing and . . . I was squirming in my seat, literally trying my best not to connect with these people. I could not handle their stories coupled with my own personal challenges of grief. I could feel my heart pounding as it was approaching my time to speak. I had no idea that we were going to have to do this. How could I?

It was soon to be my turn to speak for the first time. I could feel my face turning beet red as the heat in the room started to penetrate every inch of my body. My heart was pounding while Scott was speaking because I sensed I was next,

"Larry and I had lunch on a Friday, and he died on a Saturday," I sobbed. I could barely catch my breath. I wiped my eyes and looked around at everyone—strangers.

A man with big, brown, puppy dog eyes and a goatee broke the awkward silence. "Wow, your loss is worse than ours. We knew we might lose our spouses; they were sick. Your loss happened out of nowhere!"

I was hardly comforted by these words, and the tissue that was serving as my shield held no more space for my tears. The facilitator looked at me and spoke gently. "That is true. My loss was also sudden; I understand how you feel." For the first time since my loss started, I felt comforted; I felt understood.

After the group meeting was over, and as I walked out toward the parking lot, I could feel Scott walking behind me. I didn't dare turn around or say a word. All I could think about was how much I hated this experience, what was the fastest way home, and what I was going to say to my sister for signing me up.

The Ups and Downs of Bereavement Groups

This style of sharing the details in a group is still a common practice in many bereavement groups. It is commonly understood that sharing is part of the healing process, but what I find is that this fails to consider the impact this has on those listening. So much sadness, so much grief; it can be a lot for one person to handle.

Many bereavement groups are facilitated by social workers who have never experienced a loss of their own. Some are excellent, from what I am told, and some are just "off the beaten track." Ignorant remarks, from those who are not equipped to support this type of grief, can remain, and may haunt a griever for years.

In one of our earlier groups, James shared that his wife hung herself in the bathroom, leaving his four-year-old and seven-year-old autistic son at home alone. Now I'm thinking about my children when they were four years old and having to witness such a tragedy. Why, is it important to share these details? Again, we never know what someone is going to share. I'm not saying never share your story; I'm only suggesting that it be shared one at a time, and only with those you trust, and with those you know who are ready and equipped to hear it.

My groups are facilitated by widows and widowers who were once participants in my group. They have been professionally trained to help others, utilizing the methods and practices that worked and still work for them. They have empathy for our members knowing what this feels like firsthand. After all, they lived it. They may not know your exact grief story, but they understand the depth of your pain.

In the beginning, I too was trained to share the details in this manner, but I hated this rule, and so I changed it. When I was in training, I was taught to move my hands around while someone was sharing their grief in order not to become absorbed in each of their stories and to detach. At the beginning of facilitating groups, I would tell the members to do the same. Why should they not be able to detach as well? I later felt it was unnecessary for them to listen to ten to fifteen stories of loss and removed the detailed sharing completely.

Sharing the gruesome details of our grief does not bring us closer. It's our camaraderie that unites us through this journey, the understanding and validation that we can't find outside with others who haven't lived it. That is what connects us, and it gives us a much-needed connection with the community, a sense of belonging that we feel we lost with our loved ones.

I strongly believe we must know our audience. This is where I believe many assume it's okay to share details, but that simply isn't true. When you're telling your story to someone of how you're feeling, and they keep switching the subject, they are telling you they can't handle what you're sharing.

The grief therapist who visits our groups yearly, Dr. Norman Fried, mentioned once in a discussion that watching the news during grief can cause vicarious traumatization. It's just too much negative information for someone who is struggling. I feel this way about sharing in these groups that it's just too much negativity while we are all struggling to find some light.

It's Not Just in Your Head; It's in Your Body

Seeing Larry dead on the bedroom floor haunted me, eventually turning into an annual flashback event. I would dwell on my trauma, reproducing it with vivid images in my head. It sometimes crept up a week or two before an actual event (anniversary, birthday, holiday, etc.), continuing to aggravate the heartache right on through to the actual day. Ruminating is an awful occurrence with grief. I developed joint pains over the years from my ruminating. They still flare up when I feel overwhelmed or stressed.

Studies show that trauma affects us on a cellular level. The physicians have put me through a myriad of tests over the years, ruling out everything from lupus to rheumatoid arthritis to Lyme disease. After negative results followed by more negative results, I came to understand that my pain was like a fibromyalgia attack that none of the doctors could diagnose.

In Bessel Van Der Kolk's book, *The Body Keeps the Score*, an author and psychiatrist speaks at length regarding the connection between trauma and its effect on the human body. I recognized after reading this book that my pain would occur in January, the anniversary of Larry's death, and then flare up in June when it was my wedding anniversary and his birthday.

The physical pain triggered by the mental flashbacks, from what I read, was my body being retraumatized by my mind, as if I found Larry dead every six months. I used to think this was my day to grieve him, but I was physically hurting myself. I would start the beginning of the month by recalling all the last days of details with him, right up to his passing. I've learned how to use this awareness to alleviate the physical pain I suffered for years.

The best way to explain this is when a person goes to a doctor, and they are nervous about the visit. When the doctor takes their blood pressure, it may be elevated because they are thinking about the visit. Their thoughts are elevating their blood pressure. There could be nothing wrong with them and the doctor may wait to repeat it when they are more relaxed.

Many members shared with me the physical symptoms of their grief. Like me, they have joint pains, and or tingling down an arm, blurred vision, and stomach issues. It's always good to not ignore any physical ailments by getting checked first by your physician.

I stopped my joint pains from happening by just changing my thoughts. This is why awareness is so important. Grief needs to feel the feelings and trauma needs not to be re-lived repeatedly.

BECAUSE I LIVED IT

Shortly after Larry died, I made sure to get a complete physical. I immediately took out a life insurance policy for each of our children. Michael, our oldest, told me once that he did not think I would make it past six months.

He truly thought I would die of a broken heart.

Actress Debbie Reynolds died one day after the loss of her daughter Carrie Fisher. This does happen more often than one would have you think. Broken Heart Syndrome, or Takotsubo Cardiomyopathy, typically occurs in the elderly, but it's certainly not limited to them. We need to understand that the surge of adrenaline that enters our bodies from stress can cause a lot of medical issues. Doing things to help ourselves during this time is so important.

In the past, widows would wear all black in public—an outward sign showing their inner pain and grief. Today, there are no uniforms for grief; no way of making it clear to others that we are in pain.

Pain Is Pain

Validation is also very important with grief. I ask people in our groups not to judge or compare their losses.

I read a meme once that said, "Whether we are drowning in two feet of water or ten feet of water, we are still drowning." Everyone on the outside is already judging us plenty; we don't need judgment inside our circle.

Years in grief are not the same as years in the real world. Ten years of loss feels like three, and three years feels like a drop in the ocean. We live in conversations of the past, often relating memories to the times before our loved one died and to the times after.

I discovered, however, that no one is truly gone until we stop speaking about them. They can't die if their stories continue to be told.

CHAPTER 6

Grief Recovery: Don't Go It Alone

I did not want to be a widow. *A widow—me?* When thinking of the word "widow," I immediately visualized a little Italian lady dressed in black with a tight, pulled-back bun in her hair, black stockings, and black shoes. I was forty-two years old, size four, and full of life. I did not have one gray hair on my head; I wore leather skirts and high heels. A widow? No, not me.

Like a child having a full-blown temper tantrum, I was adamant about not wanting to be in "a group of loss." I was sure Larry would not want me to be without him; he would not want me to be in that room.

I hated every second of my life now, and as someone who was used to making her own choices, I resented that I had not made this choice.

These were thoughts, not facts. I, like many women, fell back to emotionally childish behavior.

The fact is that bereavement groups help many people with these and other issues.

I remember wanting to yell at my sister for signing me up for what I thought was nonsense. I knew she couldn't help but remember the words I wrote in a letter explaining how pointless life felt without my Larry. I was frightfully suicidal. I have also learned over the years that many have felt just like me.

The intensity of my pain was so crippling that I convinced myself our children would be better off with other family members, and so on a Saturday evening, not even three months after losing Larry, I treated myself to a dinner and a movie date for one, and when I came home, I wrote a goodbye letter, reached into my medicine cabinet, removed all the miscellaneous pills, laid them out in the palm of my hand, and I stared at them. *What if?* I thought, *What if I don't end up with Larry?*

An old movie came to my mind: *What Dreams May Come.* Robin Williams plays the husband of Annabella Sciorra's character; four years after losing both of their children in an automobile accident, Williams' character dies in an accident, as well. Unable to handle the pain, Sciorra's character dies by suicide, but she does not end up with her family; her intentional death takes her soul somewhere else (not a personal belief).

I remember watching this movie with Larry. Robin Williams searched all over hell for her, giving up Heaven, and was willing to spend eternity in hell just to be with her. While watching this scene, Larry leaned in and whispered in my ear: "I would give up Heaven for you."

Oh, my Lord, where am I? I let go of the pills, and I grabbed the phone. I paged Ella, my best friend, and at three-thirty in the morning, my phone rang. She later told me her beeper was sitting in her kitchen, on the opposite side of her house, yet she was awakened by it, and all I had to say was, "I can't do this anymore."

"I'm on my way!" She was at my house so fast, before I could even hang up the phone; from my window, I saw Ella pulling into my driveway. She picked me up, and we went to a twenty-four-hour diner, where we stayed until it was time to go to work the following morning. Ella stayed up with me in that diner all night, holding my hand and watching me as I bawled my eyes out.

Ella and Me

BECAUSE I LIVED IT

Ella lost her dad when she was nine, and her mom was thirty-six. My sudden loss was triggering her own, and she wanted to be there for me and my family however she could. We have always been there for each other—no excuses, not even death.

I told my sister the truth about what happened that night, and she flipped. "Your kids have been through so much! How could you not think of them first?"

All I could say was, "I know."

There are no words to describe the intensity of pain I was in, and there was no way she could possibly understand. It was as though I'd lost a part of my body. I couldn't fathom the possibility of being a good mother without their father, and I knew my sister would have no concept of the depth of my pain.

Understanding the Immediacy of Grief

No one understands what this is unless they have lived it. I knew my sister and the rest of my family had sympathy for me, but there was no way for them to truly empathize with the magnitude of pain I was in. Empathy comes from a place of knowing. I read this somewhere on my travels and really felt it to be true in so many circumstances.

In the book *The Grieving Brain* by Mary-Frances O'Connor, Ph.D., she describes what happens in our brain during grief, making me know it was all normal, especially for complicated grief like mine. I later did not want to kill myself; however, I had an overwhelming feeling that I just didn't want to live. I was just existing. In my groups, we take people right away following their loss, and it's because of this very reason that I do. My group is evidence-based; many have healed together.

This means that people can be accepted before the first three months, and it can help them process and go forward with support. Many have shared that our groups have saved their lives. No other group would accept them, and the comfort cannot be compared.

We recently had a very young pregnant woman whose husband was on his deathbed. We signed her up, and he passed right before we started group; my assistant, Arlene, helped her find a funeral home and assisted her with whatever she needed. She went right into our program and is grateful because no other group in our area would have taken her.

People with loss do not always seek a therapist; people call me because they know I understand their pain. How can anyone tell someone in pain that there is a three-month waiting period for help with their bereavement? I have found this to be a rule amongst many groups from my area and outside of it. I am hoping that if you are facilitating groups, you will take this into consideration when allowing people to join.

I understand the rules, but I believe that in certain circumstances, the rules are too rigid. I have accepted people as early as a week following a loss, and I ask them to repeat. In total, they have been with us for four months.

If we all know that we all grieve differently, then how could we put this rule out for everyone? Many need coping skills right away and feel secure in the group that they are not alone. If it's too soon for them, they know right away, and the door is open for two years. We all work on a volunteer basis; I am not selling anything except sincerity.

If your friend calls you and says, "I am hurting, I am having dark thoughts, and I am struggling to cope," how do you respond? Do you say, I" am sorry; you must wait three months? If they are too emotional, I might say, "If you can't speak and just want to listen and learn, that is fine," and offer for them to come sit next to me.

Personally, I have found that holding space for those grieving during those early weeks following their loss and giving them coping skills is better than leaving them in society with nothing. It is in the early days, early weeks, early months that those suicidal thoughts creep up the most. Those early weeks are especially difficult for us all, especially those who have been with their loved ones since high school or those who have had multiple losses. There are so many complicated scenarios that contribute to a person's grief.

The knowledge we learn about grief may only be known from family tradition or a friend who lost someone years ago giving you advice. That information may not be correct for you because all grief is different.

When Lauren, at only forty years old, suddenly lost her second husband, she sent me a text in the middle of the night, explaining that she didn't think she would make it till morning. We stayed on the phone, texting into the morning hours. That night, I was her Ella, and I walked her through what may have been the worst night of her life.

About Suicide

Suicide is the eleventh cause of death in the U.S (2023)[3]

"How could he kill himself when he knew I was going to be the only person who would have found him?" Jane lost her military husband by suicide, which can cause a very complicated relationship to form with our own contemplations. I explained to her that he was not thinking about that—just as I wasn't thinking about my own children on that dark night many moons ago. He needed his medication, and they had just moved to a new state. The VA hospital couldn't fill his prescription because he could not prove his new residency. On that very same day that he tried to get his medication and failed, he died by suicide.

I have noted that many of the people from our group conversations who have lost their loved one by suicide have ingested drugs or alcohol with an antidepressant. What I have also noticed over the years is that widows of suicide separate themselves from others over the thoughts about how they believe that their person died by choice and not by an illness. The person suffering from this pain did not see this as a choice. Many widows are concerned about what others will think of them. It's another form of isolation. That is only a thought, and the fact is we want to help you, and you are one of us; we help you without judgment.

---

3. "Suicide." National Institute of Mental Health. https://www.nimh.nih .gov/health/statistics/suicide. Accessed September 10, 2024.

Marilyn was married for thirty years when her husband, Joe, died by suicide. The doctors were saying that he had been mentally ill, a question many find themselves struggling with. They ask, *How is it that I have been married all these years and not aware of this diagnosis of mental illness?*

I have more widows than widowers from suicide; in conversation, many have shared that they had an argument prior to their loved one taking their lives. Now that wife or husband is carrying the guilt of the fight and the shame of the death.

My hypothesis is that they argue on purpose, possibly unconsciously, so you will be mad at them and not grieve them. Remember, they are not thinking rationally. Sometimes, the argument isn't personal; it's more about them being frustrated and angry over not being able to pull themselves out of their situation. Some of my widows have found out something from their spouse's past that the spouse was ashamed of.

This is what I have learned through years of hearing their grief stories, which have many similarities.

In many cases, something happened before you even knew them—possibly an untreated depression, alcohol and drug abuse, an undiagnosed mental illness, sexual abuse as a child, parental abuse or neglect, etc. So many sad things have been discovered after a spouse died that the surviving husband or wife knew nothing about. Of course, there are other situations where this happens, like postpartum depression and chemical imbalances. Suicide is considered an illness, not a rational decision or, in any way, a choice.

There are so many tragic deaths, many trying to survive the loss by suicide. These people need a trauma therapist and support group. Many of them feel stuck in a prison of pain and guilt. *What didn't I see? What did I do wrong? How could I have stopped this?* There is so much shame around this topic. I believe that the therapist needs specific training to help peel back the onion of what is going on for them. I recently shared a meme that said, *Suicide doesn't end the pain. It just passes it on to someone else.* This is so very true.

If you are a widow by suicide, you are a widow just like the rest of us, and your shock is equal to ours; you deserve to be loved and cared for over such a tragedy. Please stop separating yourself from us; we care about you and your pain.

On a separate note, while listening to the *Being Well* podcast, I heard Dr. Mary Francis O'Connor tell Forrest Hanson that studies are now finding that antidepressants are not always what is needed for grief. (This, of course, would be referring to someone who did not have any mental health issues prior to their loss.)

She stated that depression and grief are different. We don't always need antidepressants. Sometimes, people come to me so drugged by their primary doctors that we can't help them. I have also read it in the *Grief Recovery Handbook* by John W. James and Russell Friedman, a program that has dealt with grievers for years. They have the same stance on this.

The depression that comers with grief is a different type of depression, one that comes from a good reason: we lost our one and only, and of course, we are depressed. I recently heard

Gladys McCarey, M.D., state in her book *The Well-Lived Life* that depression stays stuck, but grief moves forward. If I felt stuck in my grief, I would try first on my own, with a therapist and a support group, before I would try taking something.

It's hard to get off once you start. Do not stop suddenly if you started already; that would not be good for your mental or physical health, and most need to be weaned off. If you haven't started but are contemplating, I would start with a low dose to take the edge off. Many general practitioners put patients on medication right away without ever mentioning the benefits of a support group or a grief therapist. We can grow around our grief, and we can live productive lives with the right support and guidance.

Is There a Timeline for Grief?

I understand now that I held on to my grief longer than I should have because I felt it kept me connected to Larry.

Many people assume others know what we need, and they do not have a clue. There are so many preconceived notions about support groups—what they offer or how they can help. "You don't know what you don't know." (One of my favorite Brooklyn-girl quotes.)

So many people choose to grieve alone without giving grief support a chance. I've had people sign up and drop out; they determine it's too soon or too late. I have found that the thoughts we tell ourselves repeatedly become our truth, yet we lack the evidence to prove it.

Support groups are fact-based in helping those who seek it. In trauma, the prefrontal cortex is compromised, as I mentioned in an earlier chapter, and so are our decision-making skills.

I tell my members this comparison with support groups and going to a gym. You may see someone in the gym who has a six-pack. However, you can't just walk in and walk out and obtain that. You must work at it daily to achieve that level of fitness. In comparison to grief, you can't go to one night of a support group and be healed. You also must work on your grief to get through this. After all, we worked on our marriages to make each other happy.

I never heard anyone say, "I woke up one day, and my grief was gone." Never!! There is no timeline. However, we can work on how we respond to what we are going through. That takes time and guidance. Do not give up on you. Most of us were never taught coping skills or how to handle grief. This is shocking because grief is a normal human experience. We were never taught how important it is to reach out when we are struggling. When death happens, we don't know where to find the right help. We hold in a lot of emotions and feelings so as not to upset others; we don't want to be that Debbie Downer in our social circle.

This is another reason why my groups have worked well. In my many years of experience as a young widow without a lot of support and then as a support group leader, I have witnessed those in my group who have shared and received so much from each other. Every member I convinced to stay thanked me later. It has truly helped them in their journey moving forward.

Letting It Out

We need to feel, we need to grieve, we need to let it all out. This pain is too much to suppress.

Journaling is my favorite modality that is often used to help with grief. I give each group member a notebook to get them started with their writing.

I believe it is so important to write about all the recent changes you have been through. Write what you were feeling during all of it. This can be especially therapeutic for caretakers whose spouses had a long-term illness, who never took time to think of themselves and their feelings, and always worried about their loved ones. They have been used to nurturing their partner and not caring for their own needs. If this is you, now you need to take care of yourself.

When you start journaling, you may feel stuck for words to help you describe your feelings. I found what helped me the most was when I would write to my husband. The words would just flow. Always be honest with yourself and what you're feeling. It helped me to write all the things I didn't have the chance to say when Larry was alive.

In *The Grief Recovery Handbook*, there are a few writing practices that may help those who have been grieving longer. There is extending forgiveness to the person if there was anything unresolved, forgiveness to yourself for anything you might have taken for granted, and apologies to your loved one and yourself for holding onto strong feelings with so much judgment on yourself. You can also write any emotional statements about your relationship. In the book, they highly recommend a confidential partner, but I did this exercise alone. I am not big on trusting anyone, so I wrote it and then shredded my letter.

I can't even describe the peace I found in writing it all out. In the end, you can say *I love you, I miss you,* and *Goodbye.* That was so big for me. I was stuck for so many years on never having the chance to say goodbye. I was also inundated with guilt from picking the doctor who ultimately killed my husband.

I ask members to write in their journals three to five things they feel grateful for. The typical response is they don't know what they feel grateful for. I respond with, "You woke up, you got dressed alone, and you drove here."

It's difficult to see what we have when we are in pain. We go into a negativity bias where we only see the negative things every day. Our grief fogs our ability to see what we do have.

Studies about negativity bias state that it's a normal human experience to feel negative after such a tragic thing happened. The amygdala of the brain is storing this information to protect us. This is part of the amygdala's function and it's why when we are traumatized, we remember all the details of what happened. This is why we get stuck in a negative thinking pattern. *If it's bad, it will happen to me,* almost like a feeling of doom.

The findings show that when we practice gratitude, it can help us stretch this part of our brain. Neuroplasticity is the ability to change the brain. We must work on this to change our mindset to be more positive about life again.

Research shows something happens when we write that simply doesn't happen when we speak. We can dig deeper into our feelings. I find this especially helpful for men who struggle with showing any emotions, always being told to be tough. The men in my generation grew up being told that men don't cry. Crying is an important release of the body's emotions.

I recently was coaching a man in his late seventies who was struggling with the loss of his wife, Sue. He had never journaled before; my coaching on writing helped him greatly. He saw how his children and grandchildren cherished everything that was once an item of Sue's.

I suggested, "Why don't you write the stories and events of your marriage, and someday your grandchildren will have this of you." It helped him change his perspective and gave him the purpose of leaving a beautiful legacy of their love; a year later, he sent me a beautiful text saying how much this suggestion helped him with his grief.

Our hope is that what others have shared, that helped them, will help us in some way. However, we must be in a place to receive it because we may not be ready. This is common with grief because one day, we are doing okay, and the next day, we feel like we are back to day one. Journaling also helps us to see the increments of recovery we are making, even if they are minimal.

Secondary Losses

I remember the first time I went food shopping after Larry had passed. I had to push myself to be the mother to our children; something that was always done instinctively was now a push. Finding the strength to go to the local supermarket was one of the many responsibilities I simply could not put on tomorrow's list.

I made it to the cash register and started placing my items on the conveyor belt. Looking up briefly, I caught sight of a short, gray-haired couple as they were walking with their cart; he had his hand on hers, making their way to their car, with their groceries, to go to their home—a home they had most likely built together, with a marriage likely longer than my Larry had lived.

Both Larry and I were short like them, and as I placed my final item down, a flood of tears immediately started falling from my eyes. I wept uncontrollably while trying to bag my groceries; as I bolted out of the store to my car, the realization that Larry and I would never grow old together overwhelmed me. How was this even possible? I didn't even process this life sentence until I saw that elderly couple and realized what I would never have.

There are so many consequences of secondary loss other than just losing our spouse. Growing old together is only one of many. Losing an income, loss of a co-parent, loss of coupled friends, loss of your go-to person, loss of your cheerleader, loss of your identity, loss of shared dreams, loss of your family unit, loss of confidence, and loss of certainty. I also feel I lost a certain amount of naivete that I will never have again.

In the beginning, there are so many moments that will catch us off guard. The supermarket can be a huge trigger, a specific aisle or a snack, a favorite piece of fruit or salad dressing—everything is a reminder. I can imagine now that shopping online can be helpful, a luxury I didn't have at the time.

I lost my Larry on January 15th; what others would never understand is that I also lost him every day after that. I lost all the everyday things he wasn't there for, that my children and I were missing. Each trigger represented another loss I had to deal with, that he was gone.

CHAPTER 7

Variations of Grief

That day I opened the door and saw Larry lying in the middle of the room, his eyes fixed and dilated, my legs were immediately like jelly as I fell to my knees, and I, without consciousness, urinated on myself. My brother-in-law, who was at my home doing work that day, rushed past me.

I looked up and saw Anthony standing in the corner of the room. He grabbed the phone immediately, and he had it pressed up against his ear, speaking with 911 in between weeping hysteria. I was now on the floor with my brother-in-law, and Larry was stretched out between us; together, we were desperately trying to perform CPR. Hearing the commotion, Danielle entered the room with my three-year-old nephew, Matthew. I screamed, "Go next door and get Matthew out of here!"

I stared at my daughter in desperation. My neighbor at the time was a doctor, and I knew my daughter knew we needed him. I kept repeating, "Please don't leave me," in between compressions and my own hysteria. His body was still warm, and I was hoping we could save him.

They took him out on a stretcher with an Ambu bag, still giving him CPR as the ambulance pulled away. We followed the ambulance, and my neighbor Jane drove me and my children. At the hospital, my neighbor's husband came out to announce to us, "We tried everything we could," but they could not save my Larry. It's a memory I wish I could forget. I kept asking myself, *How is this even possible?*

He was only forty-four.

Minutes after returning home, the phone rang, and it was someone from the hospital asking me if I wanted to donate Larry's organs. I was horrified; this was a nightmare that just wouldn't end. I screamed so loudly that they probably heard me back in Brooklyn, and I hung up the phone.

Hanging up on them like that was something I later regretted.

In the midst of the shock I felt from losing him, coupled with not knowing what his wishes would have been, the decision to donate his organs was something I could not make. Later, I put myself as a donor on my driver's license in hopes of somehow making up for what I could not do in my distress.

He was so young. He was not supposed to die. Ella brought me to my room to help me change my pants. I hadn't realized they were still soaked with urine from when I first fell to my knees. She knew people would be coming to my house. The mere thought of him dead caused me physical chest pain; I would hold my chest as I would weep.

Physical pain is not uncommon for people who are grieving. There is also an intense amount of fatigue caused by the constant thoughts that plague us.

Processing Grief

I was thinking recently about the phone call between my sister and me on the day I told her Larry had died; my sister asked me how her son Matthew was doing, and when I looked over at him, he was eating all the candy out of a dish I had on my coffee table. I was on a house phone, and he was in my eyesight as I watched him eating the candy. "He's only three," I said to my sister, reassuring her about his well-being. "He has no idea what is really happening."

We later realized that Matthew was suffering from separation anxiety and PTSD in the form of flashbacks. It wasn't until he was ten years old that he was able to articulate this to my sister—he had flashbacks of the day Larry died and of my son Michael arguing with a police officer to let him inside his home.

Unlike adults, children process things as time goes on. This was something I had zero understanding of at the time. We think a three-year-old doesn't have the capacity to remember an event so young, but the tragedy affects them through flashbacks they are later able to piece together.

I also want to mention that babies who are not even born will mourn their deceased parents. They grow up seeing other families with two parents and long for theirs.

People will say things to a young, widowed person like, "Well, at least they were too young to know," or too young to remember. That statement is not true. They know and grieve in silence.

My grandmother lost her mother during childbirth and spoke of her often, a woman she never met. She died during the depression and was never given a tombstone. At eighty years old, my grandmother told me she saved money to have one made.

I also can relate to looking at other families and wishing I had a dad, a dad who was with us in our home. My dad is really such a sweet man, and he was never abusive verbally or physically; he just wasn't around.

Grieving on Social Media

"I want my husband back" is a Facebook post I see all too often from recent widows. This, of course, is not humanly possible.

So why do some women write this? They clearly don't have the coping skills they need to deal with what they are going through. This is where therapy and support groups help.

Other social media posts I've read make me feel like I'm invading someone's privacy, like I am reading someone's personal journal of their love for their spouse. I am sure this makes other people, who don't understand grief, very uncomfortable. Of course, the grieving person doesn't care about that when they are writing, and, believe it or not, they are not looking for sympathy—they just don't know where to release all their pain.

If you are the one grieving, please know that not everyone knows how to hold space for your pain, and becoming angry at them for not understanding you is not fair to them. It's difficult to understand this loss if you haven't lived it. People like to compare widowhood to other types of loss, but they're just not the same.

So, instead of writing a love letter to your deceased spouse on Facebook, post simply, "I need help." Ask if anyone is free for coffee or simply just to talk. We sometimes don't know what we need, but I can tell you it's love, support, validation, and sometimes just someone who can listen without giving advice.

Many widows write their stories in a blog; they share the link with friends and give them a choice to listen. Social media, blogging, posting—all of this was not an option for me in my time of loss. I spent countless nights at a pity party of one, journaling privately and for only myself. I found this extremely beneficial to my healing.

It's very possible that what you're going through, and the ways you learn to cope with it, may be a help and encouragement to others. Go ahead and blog your feelings; get them out. At some point, some of your followers will start moving forward and out of the darkness themselves. When they start to find their way, a new audience will arrive.

Your support or bereavement group, if you are a part of one, is another place where you will opportunities for your story to encourage others. Our groups should be a safe space to share. I ask my members to remember the importance of compassion and to try to be patient with others, just as my facilitators and I were when they were new members. We see people evolve when they learn about other ways to get their pain out, or find the right audience who "gets" them.

I believe this is when it's important for our longer, more seasoned widows to share inspirational posts on Facebook to help those who are struggling—not to judge them on how they grieve, but to help them. We can judge someone who's too sad or happy too soon, someone who wants to date, or someone young who chooses never to date. The reality is that everyone must grieve in their own way, and there is no wrong way. If someone seems like they have it together, that would be the person I would be so curious to know how.

The famous psychiatrist Bessel Van Der Kolk, on the *Very Well Mind* podcast (episode 236) with Amy Morin, said, "Ask someone who has survived the same trauma as you and how they got through it," because that person's strategy just may work for you. I loved what he said because that is exactly what I believe happens in groups.

I watched an interview on Oprah's "Soul Series" about a woman, Madonna Badger, who lost her parents and her three little girls in a house fire. How does anyone survive that? She was divorced, and her boyfriend accidentally didn't put the embers out after cleaning out the fireplace. Where does one go when they lose so much?

She shared with Oprah how she got on with her life. She said love and her faith saved her. Her closest friends never left her side. She took that energy and now goes and speaks at high schools about resilience.

Not All Grief Is the Same

We are all in the same storm, but we are not all in the same boat. This pain and suffering taught me how to be more empathetic toward anyone in pain.

Many friends and family do not know how to handle the pain we are in. I have learned over time that they are tortured by their desire to help without knowing how. We must give them options to know how to help us, and we, in turn, can find ways to help others.

A memory of my own experience of grieving Larry's death comes back to me:

> *It's Wednesday night again, and I am back in my group. It has been eight weeks of meetings. Another week has passed, and another week has arrived. The weeks have flown by, and the world has carried on; everyone's life has moved on but mine. I am back in that circle with nothing else to do; the nights are long and lonely. How can it be that the sun rises and sets, and Larry is nowhere to be found?*

I remember the feelings so clearly. Widowhood is an incredibly strange experience. I could not understand how I could feel so lonely in a crowded room. Loneliness is truly one of the most difficult emotions to experience. I had my kids, my sisters, my mom, my dad, Ella, and my friends, but my loneliness was all around the fact that there was no longer any contact with my Larry. It was intense.

Loneliness is different from solitude; the cure for loneliness is connection. They say loneliness can be harmful to your mental health as well as physical health. I've heard that research indicates loneliness is equal to smoking fifteen cigarettes a day! Taking steps to connect with people will help you to feel better. Fear of connecting can keep you as a prisoner. In our support groups, what works is that we all understand the pain of losing our person.

I have a memory of speaking with someone one day, and as we were speaking, he kept touching my forearm. When he did that, I stopped hearing what he was saying to me, though he was only inches away; all I heard was blah, blah, blah, and my focus was fixated on my arm. It had been so long since anyone had touched me, I noted.

One evening in the "Cuckoo's Nest," one man shared that he threw out "all his wife's crap." I hadn't even moved Larry's slippers. His glasses were exactly where he had left them— sitting on my night table. For months, I picked them up, dusted them, and placed them back as though he would come back home. This man in my group is proudly throwing away his wife's things, calling them crap, and using up our time to explain everything he hated about her. Everything about Larry's things was sacred to me. I was clinging to everything like it was gold— even his toothbrush and the last piece of soap he used.

It is extremely common for widows and widowers to hang on to their spouse's things and to associate their person with a material item. One man was so comforted by his wife's perfume that he sprayed it on his own clothing each morning.

Many people will wear their spouse's clothing. I believe that there is no set time when anyone should get rid of anything. We know when we are ready. Their belongings are a part of them, so we attach ourselves to their belongings. For many, this is how they grieve. I will write more about this later.

Dealing with Children's Grief

My younger sister found a bereavement group for my kids on Thursday nights. While the kids were in groups, parents had to wait in a big room, unable to leave in case one of our children had a panic attack and needed our help. This was not a typical bereavement group for the loss of a parent; there were children who suffered all kinds of loss—some lost a father, a mother, a grandparent, or even a sibling.

I persuaded Anthony, my fourteen-year-old son, to go for his sister Danielle. She was eleven, and I begged Anthony to go for her; even if he didn't need it, she needed him to go to get the help. I said the same thing to Danielle, and the two of them loved each other enough to go together. Neither Danielle nor Anthony ever told me what they did while in that room. I was just happy if, in some way, it would help them with the loss of their father.

Years later, while attending therapy as a young adult, Anthony discovered that because he felt he went to this group for his sister, he never shared properly, or with intent, for himself. In retrospect, my plan backfired. I have now learned that we cannot force teenagers to go to therapy if they don't want to. We can lead by example, but this marks yet another challenge we have as the solo parent.

One day, while cleaning Anthony's room, I found matches and a candle on his dresser. I panicked, thinking he was going to burn my house down, and immediately threw them away. Later, I found out that it was a memory candle he had made in his bereavement group.

My guilt overcame me. How could I have known? I felt like I couldn't handle his grief on top of my own.

Our ability to communicate was shattered by the pressure of our grief, yet I failed to realize this because of the fog that surrounded me. Like my own childhood, my children lost their father and their mother at the same time; I was mentally and emotionally unavailable to them.

Larry wore a gray sweater the day before he died. I kept it in my closet, and I would lay with it in bed at night. It was the only item of clothing that still had Larry's scent, and I treasured it. One afternoon, I went to get it, and it was nowhere to be found. I searched my closet frantically and started to break down. The kids came home from school, and I saw right away that Anthony was wearing his sweater—Larry's sweater—and I lost it.

"How dare you take that out of my closet!" I yelled and screamed at him to take the sweater off, ripped it from his hands, and ran with it to my bedroom, where I collapsed on my bed in a pile of tears. The smell was gone, and it made Larry's absence even more unbearable. I felt like it was the only piece of Larry I still had left until I realized how foolish I was being. My child, Larry's child, is half of Larry's flesh and blood, and here I am, clinging to a damn sweater with cologne on it. What was wrong with me? I felt like I was losing my mind.

As I was crying, it dawned on me that my son, like me, wanted to hang on to this piece of his dad. I realized I was hogging it all for myself. I pulled myself together, and I brought his father's sweater to his son. I apologized and told him I realized what he was feeling. I gave him the sweater, and I held him as he wept in my arms.

We cannot beat ourselves up for what we do. There was no guide on how to handle a fourteen-year-old in grief.

I have spoken with and apologized to each of my children for the days that were taken from them by my grief when I couldn't be there for them like I always was. My therapist had said that my apology could potentially remove a layer of their trauma. That made me think of the fact that my father never apologized, but I can imagine that if he ever did, it would have meant a lot to my sisters and me.

My sons both said to me," Mom, you were always the best," but when I said it to Danielle, her eyes welled up, and a tear fell to her cheek. I knew I hit a nerve. I worked on re-establishing my relationship with my daughter, driving to Queens every week to have a day together. I believe an apology should be backed up with a change of behavior.

We can't redo the past, but we can work on our relationships going into the future. I work on my relationships with all my kids. I learn what they like and don't like and try to be there for them whenever they reach out.

I'm not quite sure why I was so attached to Larry's things, except for the fact that they were part of him, and I didn't want any part of him to be erased, especially when nothing new would ever come from him again. All my photos of Larry are the same, and I just keep posting them yearly. I think only someone who has experienced this would understand.

I know many others feel just as I had. Recently, a member, Jean, called me about selling her husband's car. She was worried about forgetting the memories they made in it, but I assured her that memories are remembered where they are written. I encouraged her to take photos and write all her memories down if she was so concerned. The memories stay in our hearts forever. I think many of us who have lived through a big loss also find it difficult with anything else that feels like a loss.

◇◇◇

Recently, I found a photo of me with my daughter on the day of her Confirmation—four months after Larry died and the first of many bittersweet occasions of her childhood. She was practically holding me up, and I could barely smile.

Raising my children without their dad was always mixed with emotions. Every birthday, every graduation, every award ceremony, every marriage and wedding, and birth—every special event was missing one very important person—my Larry.

Danielle at 11, at her confirmation

Danielle, 11, Michael, 18, and Anthony, 14. This photo was taken at our last Christmas party before Larry died.

As the earth continued to revolve around the sun, I felt like I could feel it physically moving—moving forward without him. In my mind, I tried to imagine him still here, but in an invisible form, one I could still feel though I could not see. The celebrations were some of the most difficult occasions; the passing of time just made me miss his presence even more, especially the births of each of my beautiful grandchildren. Each of these events activated my grief.

CHAPTER 8

Wednesdays

I learned that not all therapists, support groups, and grief are created equal. The children's group took place on a Thursday night. While my kids were in their group, I sat in the waiting room downstairs. A female moderator sat quietly while people spoke.

As soon as I walked in, whom did I see but Scott? "Wow, you're here too?" I was surprised that we were meeting again. He smiled, and I found an empty seat directly across from him. Before I sat down, I turned my head quickly, looking back, and caught him red-handed, looking me up and down. *Was he just checking me out?* I smiled at him, but the gesture actually made me nervous; I was totally not ready for something like that.

There was a man sitting in the back of the room who had been widowed for only one week. "I know it's only been one week, but I started dating." I was absolutely shocked. One week after his wife's death, and he was dating? I found myself judging him and questioning whether this guy ever loved his wife to begin with. I mean, how could he? There were days that I could barely get out of bed.

Then he said, "I am not going to spend another day feeling sorry for myself. One thing my wife's death taught me is that life is too short." I had to agree with that last statement, but seriously? *Wow*, I thought. It had only been one week! Were the funeral flowers even dead yet?

I have learned that men and women think very differently when it comes to grief. Most men seem to have the ability to compartmentalize most, not all. I've also learned to try not to judge others. We all have our own journey.

One thing, however, is that many men have shared with me that they subsequently entered relationships only to discover, years later, that they were not compatible but simply feared being alone.

What I find sad is that many men, the ones I have known, don't even give themselves a chance to figure out who they are without their spouses before jumping into a relationship with someone new. Taking some additional time could save some additional heartbreak. Again, I do not intend to judge; I'm just reflecting what I have heard over the past seventeen years. Honestly, I feel sorry for the women they are dating. Many of them get hurt.

Scott and I joked about this guy and his mad dash to get a new wife. We also joked about the other guy from our other group who threw out all his wife's "crap."

Scott looked at me and said, "I loved my wife," and my heart broke a little more. We were grieving similarly because we were not angry with our spouses for dying; we both loved them dearly.

During the break, a young woman approached Scott and me and said, "I just want a warm body and an income." I spit out my water. What made us so different from these people? We were shocked by what we were hearing.

I started looking forward to Wednesdays and Thursdays, to seeing Scott and sharing different stories and challenges we had to deal with in our widowhood. His loss was only five months before mine, and we were dealing with similar things at similar times.

I remember asking Scott if he and Sally ever spoke about what he would do after her death. He said neither of them ever expected her to die. Innocently, I said, "But you knew she had cancer."

"It was contained," he said. "They were supposed to remove the tumor, and she was supposed to be okay." Even on the feeding tube, no one said she was going to die.

"There was always hope." He had a sad look on his face, and I stared deeply into his dark brown eyes. I could feel his pain, and I remember thinking that even though Sally had been sick, he felt just like me. His loss was also sudden. There was a heaviness in my chest, and I realized that it is possible for all losses to feel like they are sudden.

Many people often feel their person didn't have to die. Even people who have cancer are never told that they will not make it until they won't.

As a caregiver after loss, there is no one to care for, and with that task being taken away, they are often left to feel that they are without purpose.

Many people survive cancer; there is always hope. However, it has been made clear to me through many of my members that sudden loss and long-term illness are both traumatic in their own ways. Regardless of how someone leaves us, their absence is what leaves us grief-stricken.

The Last Night of the Group

It was June 2000, and my bereavement group was meeting for its final night. We had completed the eight weeks together, although I believe I was only half in and not the way I should have been, missing many of the meetings. We all participated in a beautiful candle ceremony, and I was moved by it in a deeper way than I thought I would be. The ending of our group was another loss in and of itself, and there was no continued connection plan put into place.

I wanted to stay connected with the few members I had become closer to. We exchanged phone numbers and decided to continue meeting weekly. I felt so strongly about staying connected with others who understood me. I suppose I had it in me from the beginning.

I knew I was fighting this widowhood thing, and I also knew of a widow from my town whom I saw from time to time—always with the same friends, who were a married couple. I wanted more for myself. I did not want to be a third wheel with my friends who were couples; in fact, when I was with those coupled friends, it was more obvious how alone I truly was.

I saw my girlfriends during the day for lunch, but I avoided restaurants I had frequented with Larry. This, I called my survival mode.

I still felt extremely lonely, and I was frequently crying. After twenty years of marriage, an eight-week bereavement group wasn't cutting it. I needed more help. I needed more support from others who understood what I was going through, not therapy from a woman who slept through my sessions nor from anybody else who had no experience with this pain.

I now realize that my grief prevented me from giving therapy a second chance. I immediately grouped all therapists into one category and was turned off by all of them because of my one experience and the heavy fog that clouded every decision. I see similarities in those who enter my group and are also struggling with connections with others.

I decided to join another bereavement group, but this time, I signed myself up. It was across town, in the same place where my kids had gone.

Most groups end after eight weeks, leaving those grieving to figure "it" out. Because of my own experience, in my groups, we help members to continue by giving them a room to meet, and we encourage them to meet virtually.

One person is picked from each group to be the "captain" (typically someone who is longer out from their loss and someone who is a bit more upbeat). No pressure. We realize everyone is grieving. We also choose a "co-captain," just in case the captain cannot or does not want to fulfill the position. Anyone can step up at any time if either of these two people fails to keep the group together. The purpose of this is to create a routine, to send emails as to when and where the group will meet, and to keep the connection strong. Many group captains have done a wonderful job of keeping their group together for years and years. They create names for their groups. Some of them called themselves Widow Warriors, New Beginnings, Fridows, and the Dows, just to name a few.

The continuation aspect of our groups is one that stands out amongst the rest.

One member told me that she joined five groups before she came to mine. It was with mine that she was able to find her road to healing. I understand how important this continued connection is; many of us have very little to no social life that is not composed of couples. We hate being different, and we need each other.

Charity walk with support group members

Group Night

Since we no longer met with the whole bereavement group on Wednesdays, Scott, the other widower from our group, and I kept up the tradition by meeting at a different restaurant every Wednesday night to share our weekly stories, mostly about our children. When I would repeat them to my friends, they always seemed funnier than when they were actually happening.

One night, Scott shared a story not involving his kids but instead about a divorced woman whom he had stopped dating after only a few months. He said she was still insisting on coming around. He booked a trip to Florida for himself and his children, and he found out that she booked a trip to Florida on her own for the same exact time. He was angry, but he had no idea what to say or do.

I told him that it was more than likely that she would make a play for him in Florida unless he clearly stated some boundaries. Before dinner was over that night, he had somewhat of a plan, and she had a new nickname: gum on your shoe.

Scott was not my type at all, but his honesty and kindness—his love for Sally—was making me feel closer to him. At my suggestion, he shaved his big Geraldo Rivera mustache, and I noticed he had dimples when he smiled. He was definitely starting to grow on me.

Five months after my loss, the new group I had joined started. Of course, I was running late again, and when I entered the room, about ten older women in their sixties sat in a circle of folding chairs in a dark and dingy room. *Oh, here we go again,* I thought, *One Flew Over the Cuckoo's Nest.*

Now, I was feeling very apprehensive. again , each member shared the gory details of their loss, and I was once again crying over their stories. Again, I thought, "Why was this necessary?"

After one woman shared the details of her loss and explained everything she saw upon finding her husband after he had fallen off a ladder, I had officially heard enough! I stood up and asked, "Who made these rules?" Like my son Michael, I walked out of the meeting and declared that these groups couldn't help me and that no widow could have ever created this!

I sobbed heavily all the way home. Sharing those details with total strangers felt like a setback, and I started wondering what Larry would do if the roles were reversed. It felt like there was a crack in the system, and I was falling right through it. This was the night I told myself, *If I ever get through this, I am going back.*

In my groups, members are separated by age. I never would have paired a forty-two-year-old woman with a group of sixty or seventy-year-olds and hoped that they would find something in common. We have groups that are separated into those with young children, those with older children, and those with no children at all. I have been told by many of my members that they are grateful we do not share the details of loss, especially by those who have had experiences with different groups. They also tell me that many groups have rejected them because of the lack of time that has passed since their loss; many were deemed "too soon."

Many of my members have young children to think about; they didn't realize there was a timeline for group support!

Although we have become so busy, I have made two years the cut-off time. I unfortunately cannot fit in everyone who calls. I believe if you can, the earlier you get into a support group, the better, because you learn how to help yourself, you don't create bad habits in coping, and you make connections that help you get through.

When registering to join my groups, many members share details with me over the phone. I am okay with validating what they are feeling. I can handle listening to them and the details of their loss, one at a time, as I am now, of course, in a different place than I was years ago.

CHAPTER 9

Normal in My Not-So-Normal Life

That September, I purchased my first computer. Scott and the other man in our group were trying to teach me how to work it and how to send emails. After several attempts, I finally learned the importance of the dot in .com.

It seems ridiculous now, but as a housewife, I had no reason to email anyone; all I had to do was call. Sometimes, late at night, when I couldn't sleep, I would send Scott an email just to pass the time and to avoid the screaming silence of my empty room. Since calling is not an option during certain hours of the night, emailing gave me the ability to connect.

I thanked Scott and the other guy by making a home-cooked meal of macaroni and meatballs, my signature dish since the early days of my marriage. My kids met Scott and the other widower for the first time that evening. It was nice having them over. It felt normal in my not-so-normal life.

Learning how to send emails and navigate Instagram, Facebook, and Zoom have all been very intimidating, but I push myself to learn, and I must say I am a quick learner when things are shown to me. I learned that I had to come out of my comfort zone, and now I teach others how to do the same.

Many women have shared with me that even driving on the parkway or having to make a left turn was overwhelming. Some of us are totally lost when we lose our spouses.

Now, with Zoom and virtual bereavement groups, I am often in a position where I must Facetime with new members to teach them what to do if they cannot meet in person. There are so many new ways to connect with others. We just must realize it's the fear that stops us from learning.

It is so hard to understand someone else's fear. Everything new is scary until we face it. Whatever we accomplish serves as a huge sense of empowerment.

I painted a quote on the wall above my desk that says, "Every great accomplishment was at first impossible." This helped me to push through whenever doubt crept in.

Changing of the Seasons

Scott, the other man, and I had officially known each other for nine months, and our friendships were growing. The other man from our group asked me if I would go with him to a movie; up until that point, it had always been the three of us.

"Movies?" I took a hard swallow as a million thoughts rushed through my mind, including, *What if anyone sees us out together?* No one would know we were only friends; after that thought popped up, I kindly declined. I was not ready for something like that, and he said he understood.

The seasonal changes always made me miss Larry more. The smell of the fall leaves and the cool, crisp, fall air started sifting in, and he wasn't there. I did not realize this would trigger some self-pity, but with the changing of the seasons, I could feel the world growing old without Larry. I guess the fog was lifting a bit because I could not remember feeling the spring and summer as strongly as I did the fall. I felt it more strongly as the new year came, and I struggled with the impending holidays. How was I going to have a holiday without my Larry?

I am not the only one to be triggered by the changing seasons. Our bodies know when something is coming close, and we can feel the pain before we even realize why. Many members have shared with me days when they felt "off," only to realize later that the day was significant of a diagnosis.

The holidays are always extremely difficult. One member, Mary, lost her husband on Christmas Day, but she shared with me once that this day wasn't the most difficult. She always knew she would be surrounded by her family, and that proved to be comforting for her.

Mary helped me to see things from a perspective I never saw before. On the anniversary of Larry's passing, I typically surrounded myself with my sister or Ella. Surrounding yourself with people you love on the day you lose your loved one is sometimes the only thing that will help you get through.

We always loved the holidays. I remember wanting to go to sleep and not wake up until January 16th, the day following the one-year anniversary of Larry's death.

When children are involved, not wanting to celebrate the holidays or a birthday is not an option. Your children want to celebrate with you, and holidays are often something that makes them happy. I struggled with this, and I made sure to share this with my members who had children.

We get one chance in our childhood, and mine was broken by the circumstances of my father's abandonment. Your children, and mine, have also lost a parent.

In every group, I share this one important statement: "Your children only have one childhood, and it has already been compromised."

I only wish I had realized this earlier; I was living through a fog, and the lack of resources kept me from moving through my grief. I made so many mistakes. I wish I had worked less and spent more quality time with my kids; they grew up so fast.

My grief and your grief pull us away from our children. It's a forced effort to do happy things when we feel sad, but children desperately need this. They lost a parent, and the other parent isn't acting like the parent that they've been familiar with since their birth.

Our first holiday was completely different from how it had been in the past. I could not bring myself to do anything as we had; it was simply too painful, but when I saw that Ella helped Danielle put a small Christmas tree in her room, I realized that she needed Christmas, and it was still my job to let her have it.

Some of my members do the same things they have always done. Some travel, getting away from it all. We all approach holidays differently; there is no rule book. I have realized the importance of having a plan. Do not let the holidays come without being prepared. One example that has worked for many is driving yourself to a holiday event so that you can leave if you feel like you're overwhelmed by your emotions. The strategies we put into place will help us to get through.

Open School Night

It was the fall of 2001, and that meant school was starting for my two younger children. I had one son in high school, my daughter was in middle school, and I had to attend open school night at two different schools. I could not believe that I had to do this all by myself.

Walking through the halls of Danielle's school and bumping into the parents Larry and I knew from when our kids were younger was an absolute nightmare.

In the distance, I saw two women talking. As I passed them, I overheard one say to the other, "She is the one whose husband dropped dead!" I pretended not to hear it but felt so hurt as I realized I was the topic of their gossip. As I continued walking, I felt every pair of eyes looking at me, and in my mind, what I had just overheard was playing like a record on repeat.

I felt ostracized, and walking through the school was a huge trigger. It brought me back to the days of my youth in Catholic school as the only child with parents who were getting a divorce—the only child with a father who committed infidelity. I was taken aback to a time with feelings I was not prepared to face.

At that time, I had my sisters, who also felt the same abandonment. Just like with my children, our communication was severed by the pain. We never discussed our feelings until we were adults. Back then, we just dealt with being ostracized by the other children and the rejection from their parents, who never let their kids come over to our home to play.

Years later, I tried EMDR therapy. Eye Movement Desensitization Reprocessing is a non-invasive method of going into unconscious memories of your past traumas to see if they are contributing to your present struggles. An old memory came back of an altercation I had with a nun. I was in fourth grade, around ten years old; I recalled how she would show favoritism to the children whose parents were able to drive her to visit her mother on Long Island. I was useless to her because my mother worked, and my parents were divorced. The EMDR enabled me to see the children from my past and the way they looked at me. I became aware of just how dirty I had felt and all the emotions of shame I had suppressed.

There was an incident once when I needed to use the restroom. I was raising my hand, and my teacher told me to put my hand down. I tried to wait for her to finish, but I couldn't hold it. I got up and went next to her and politely asked," Please, Sister, may I please use the bathroom? It's an emergency."

Because I had interrupted this nun while she was teaching, she pulled her arm back behind her shoulder and slapped me with a hard wallop in front of all my classmates. I was knocked off my feet by the shock of it all, causing me to release and urinate all over myself. I was ashamed and mortified in front of an entire classroom and my peers.

During the EMDR flashback, I could smell the urine of the wet wool of my uniform skirt, which brought the entire incident back to life for me. After a while, she sent me to the restroom so I could clean myself, and when I returned, I remembered that she had put her arm around my waist, something I yearned for. She was showing me what I thought was affection for the first time. She then told me not to mention this to my mother, that my disobedience and interruption would certainly make her upset. At ten years old, I was manipulated by a nun into believing that I deserved to be slapped for needing to use the bathroom.

I never told anyone about this experience; up until this EMDR flashback, I took full responsibility for the situation and thought I deserved what had happened. I shared this with my sisters, and my older sister confirmed that she, too, had been made to feel dirty. I cried for two days, which I thought was strange, but I had suppressed this unworthiness and shame for so long that I guess I needed to cry for the little girl I once was. My therapist helped me to recognize that I did not create the circumstance I was in. I take comfort in the relationships I have nurtured with nuns today. They have taught me that not all people, including nuns, are the same.

Through this type of therapy, EMDR, many people can recover from trauma and other distressing life experiences, including PTSD, anxiety, depression, and panic disorders. There is also EMDR with tapping that helped me heal from the early trauma of my father's abandonment. It's strange, because he was back in my life for years, but what happened during my childhood still affected me as an adult.

However, this technique needs a rescue after. We can get very emotional and need a safe place or person to connect with when completed. I can't stress this enough.

Many people fail to realize how our past affects the way we feel about ourselves in the present. To alleviate some of these traumas was incredibly emotional, but it was also freeing, as I was finally able to recognize how much I was suppressing and how distorted my view of myself was. I also feel that Larry's adoring love helped push this away. The words we say and the way we act as adults have much to do with the way we were treated as children.

EMDR has helped many people who have suffered multiple losses or those who feel stuck in their trauma. Sometimes, those feelings of being stuck stem from hidden traumas, just as mine did. I've noticed that some of my members ,who also suffered childhood traumas, often suffer in a more complex way with their grief. I keep saying we all grieve differently because we never truly know the full circumstances of a person's history before the loss.

To understand more about EMDR, I read the book *Every Memory Deserves Respect*, written by Michael Baldwin and Deborah Korn, PsyD. It may help you to understand the technique more clearly. This book is available on Audible.

Back to Open School Night

There were no warning signs as I was moving through my life after losing Larry. There was no road map that warned me about what was ahead, and I had no idea how painful going to an "open school night" could possibly be.

I floated from classroom to classroom, desperately trying to hold back my tears with a lump in my throat. My feelings of loneliness grew stronger with each couple I passed or had to sit beside. I saw so many familiar faces that I couldn't help but feel like I looked different to them because half of me was gone.

Sometimes, adults can be so insensitive to others' pain. Parents whom I knew a little better came right up to me to ask how I was, and all I felt like saying was, "How do you think I am? My husband is dead." Of course, I didn't say that.

Others would say, "I can't imagine," and I would confirm that they could not. I started to question if they wanted me to describe my pain so they could imagine it.

∞∞

People who are grieving are extremely sensitive. I am so careful not to ask my members, "How are you?" I ask them, "How are you doing today?"

There is a huge difference.

I must admit that if you looked at me, my hair was always done, my makeup was always on, and I was always dressed nicely—no one would ever be able to see my pain through my façade. Most people continue to groom out of habit, and I think others perceive this means that, in some way, we are okay. Robin Williams always had a smile on, yet now we clearly know that he struggled with depression. Even though I was dressed nicely, I was dying inside and wanted to be buried with Larry.

Just when I felt like leaving, I ran into the one person who understood me, and I was briefly saved by Scott. Brett, his oldest son, and my youngest, Danielle, were the same age. Together, we walked to the lunchroom where there was to be a speech. As we walked, I shared with him how I hated running into so many people. Scott admitted that he was happy that he worked all day and barely knew anyone.

In the lunchroom, the teacher speaking must have been nervous because he couldn't keep his gaze off of the ceiling above him. "Watch the speaker," I whispered to Scott. He was just not as visual as I am; Scott barely noticed, but once I brought it to his attention, it only took about two minutes to elapse before both of us were giggling uncontrollably.

We were like teenagers in high school, tears streaming down our faces from desperately trying to stifle our hysterical laughter. Every time we thought we had our laughter under control, we would look up, and the teacher would be looking at the ceiling again. I found this to be so hysterical that I had to get up and walk out of the room to compose myself.

It felt good to have a friend to laugh with, free from judgment—especially after the tension I had felt that night. For the first time in a long time, I felt more like the old me, laughing at things with someone I truly felt was a friend.

Sometimes, you can forget what happiness feels like when you're smothered in so much sadness.

We can laugh and grieve at the same time.

People who are not grieving think we can't laugh or find something funny; even my groups think this until I share this story of Larry's wake and my eleven-year-old daughter.

During Larry's wake, his mother was draped over his coffin, crying, "Talk to me, talk to me." She kept repeating it over and over. My eleven-year-old daughter and I were standing beside her, grief-stricken.

My daughter proceeded to twist her mouth to the side and, in a different voice like a parrot, said, "Hello!"

I instantly started to laugh and asked a friend to take me out of the room. I just didn't expect it at that moment, and it struck me not just as funny but hysterical. It was a human response. I was still devastated that he was gone.

My First Job

Before Larry died, I started painting some faux finishes and murals in our home. I learned a few simple techniques from a short, two-hour workshop, and I started painting for family and friends part time.

Larry did not want me to work. He came from that old-school mindset, fearing what people would assume about his ability to support me financially. I argued that it wasn't about the money; it was giving me so much pleasure in letting my creativity flow. The response from clients made me feel talented and valued.

We compromised. I called it my "shoe money." I started at nine and worked till around two or two-thirty. I had to be home by three o'clock, just in time to greet Danielle as she got off the school bus. My jobs were small. I was painting a mural in a baby's nursery or faux painting a powder room.

After Larry died, I didn't paint for over a year. I lost any following I may have had, and I was looking for work. I asked friends and acquaintances if they knew of anything I could do full time or even part time. I needed an income, and I needed it quickly.

A man named Marsh, who knew my story, hired me to do some filing for an insurance agency. I told Marsh that I had not worked in a long time but that I was planning on opening a painting business. While I worked for Marsh, I tried to put together a small portfolio of my work, and I made business cards that I displayed at local paint stores. Painting was all I could do to earn money. Going back to my job as a respiratory technician would require going back to school for more credits, and going back to school was out of the question. I had bills to pay and three children to raise.

After about three months of working for Marsh, my painting business was starting to take off. Filing papers was never my forte; I literally had to recite the entire alphabet in my head every time I had another document to file. He was so kind to hire me, but sadly, I'm certain he is still looking for some of his files to this day.

To repay Marsh for giving me a job when I was desperate, I painted a room in his home, and I officially started my own full-time decorative painting business in the fall of 2002. I registered with the state, opened a business checking account, and pulled the back seats out of my old minivan to create my very own makeshift travel painting shop. I had milk crates filled to the brim with paints and brushes and drop cloths, and before I knew it, I was booked three months in advance.

While doing a job in one area, I would get two or three more from my clients' friends and neighbors. I never had to advertise, and I estimated the time needed for each job by meeting with each client and physically looking at the room they wanted me to paint. If ever I finished a job early, I took the day as a day of rest before moving on to the next one. I painted sample boards for each job and quoted the client a specific rate. I felt like I was coloring in a coloring book and getting paid for it.

I named my business "Strokes of Creativity," branching off into more creative directions by offering window treatments and carpeting. Eventually, I had to hire people because the work simply became too much

My new business

101

for one person, and I charged more as more jobs came to provide my employees with their salaries. I always found it funny that my employees had master's degrees, and I had never gone to college. I also have to say my mother was wrong about me making a living from my art.

I learned what it meant to operate a business from Larry, and I knew that I couldn't fail because my children were depending on me.

The only problem was that I was always working; it was like history was repeating itself. Like my mother, I was never home, but now I understood the same fear she must have felt about being able to keep a roof over our heads and food on the table. I refused to take away anything my children had when their father was still alive. This was why I worked every day and every night. I drafted estimates and put together sample boards between loads of laundry and cooking dinner. My fear of financial hardship kept me from getting any real rest.

I received a bill that I wasn't prepared to pay, and that same evening, I received a call to give an estimate. The job involved marbleizing all the columns in a church. The night before I was to provide the estimate, I watched a video on marbling, something I had not done before. I went in there with confidence, which ultimately landed me the job. It came out beautifully, and I surprised myself; that was the impetus to start taking art classes, which was my first introduction to schooling in decorative painting.

The work was backbreaking, and all my years of training in the gym were paying off. I had to carry heavy ladders and

It was backbreaking work.

buckets; I climbed scaffolds and climbed over refrigerators, and in the cold winter, I had to carry all my paints, piled in heavy crates, in and out of my house daily so they wouldn't freeze.

One particular estimate has always stood out in my memory. It was a cold winter night. After working all day, I rushed our dinner and grabbed my portfolio to do an estimate. The night estimates were what provided the day work. We didn't have GPS navigation back then and I would have had to follow written instructions in the dark, pulling over several times to get my bearings. I was physically and mentally exhausted.

When I arrived, I rang the doorbell. A man answered the door, whom I assumed to be the husband, and as I walked past their kitchen into the warm den where I was directed, a fire was crackling. I could smell the aroma of the dinner they'd just eaten. It was a warm and inviting home and the husband sat next to his lovely wife on the couch. This estimate was unusual because the women alone would typically be my customer. But this couple were a team.

The warmness of the room and the way they were looking at my samples together just made me want to cry. I felt envious; I don't think I had ever felt this emotion as an adult. I cried in my car on the way home. A Donna Summers song came on the radio and the lyrics, "I will never have that recipe again," were the backdrop to my tears.

We didn't have Facebook back then and today many members will tell me they feel envious when they scroll through their Facebook, seeing couples smiling or families together. It always makes me think of that night.

Remember: we can avoid Facebook or not scroll. There are choices we can make to help ourselves. (I also feel every smiling face in a photo is not always authentic to what is really going on!)

Three Years and Counting

It was during a snowy winter that I found myself close to my breaking point. I remember it was three years after Larry passed. I was shoveling out the entire driveway, and my overalls were soaked. I had to change again before starting my workday. I was exhausted before my day even started. I fell to my knees and wept in my driveway. I remember looking up toward Heaven and asking God why he hated me so much. The responsibilities were overwhelming me, and the snow was burying me beneath them all.

I guess after a few years passed, people assumed I was okay, and they no longer looked at me like I was a widow. Perhaps it was because I was dating, but Scott had his own house and children to tend to, and he could not be at mine in the early morning hours when I would have needed him. My house and my kids were all my responsibility. Nothing fell on him. I think people assume that after a few years, a widow is back to normal life, which is not true. I still didn't have a husband, and I wasn't capable of doing everything my husband did.

As New Yorkers, we struggle with seasons, especially when the cold winter months hit and the snow starts to fall. I always think of my widows. I seek out anyone I know in their area, who has a plow or a snowblower, who can help them if needed. Things like this were always so overwhelming for me, and I will never forget how miserable those days were.

Widowhood is equivalent to many years of doing things solo, and the snow was always my reminder. I remember sharing my discontent with winter with my groups, saying, "I always felt angry when it snowed. If I shared it with my groups who met in the spring, their laughter quickly turned into statements of confirmation when the winter months came along. It was one more thing that we had to be responsible for, that our husbands had once taken care of.

In 2003, I suffered from severe tendonitis in my right elbow because of all the painting I was constantly doing. I called it "faux bo," wrapped it with an ace bandage, and kept painting through the pain. I couldn't afford to take off. I faux-painted right up to Christmas Eve, leaving very little time for a social life. I started to create designs and sell my ideas. Decorators hired me, and painters were making money from my talent.

I was proud of myself for creating this successful business on my own, and after a few years, I had saved enough money for a work truck with ladder racks. Scott was so impressed with my transition from being a housewife to filing for Marsh to now owning and operating my own painting business that he became my biggest cheerleader. He co-signed for me on the truck, since I was still establishing credit, and his words of affirmation and support helped me get through some of the more difficult business blues.

If Larry ever came back to Earth, I felt he wouldn't have recognized me. Every day, I learned how much I was capable of, and it was more than I ever previously imagined. Things like this made me believe that God knew there would be a time in my life when I was going to need to paint, and it has always caused me to reflect this quote by Emma Bombeck: "When I stand before God at the end of my life, I would hope that I would have not a single talent left and could say, 'I used everything you gave me.'"

I have met many widows with talents they never would have tapped into as a resource to help them bring in an income. One woman was an incredible singer, and after years of working

222222

a desk job, she was no longer being fulfilled. Finally, she was convinced to start using her voice, and it wasn't before long that she started singing in restaurants, earning enough money to support herself. Sometimes, the only thing holding us back is ourselves.

The Tickets

I once had a job that required me to paint four angels on a ceiling. I learned from one of the workshops I had taken that using an appliqué would save me both the time and neck pain that would have resulted from hours of drawing with my head stretched up, and my body twisted to get the right angle. All I had to do was paint with a particular primer and rub on the appliqué, touching up whatever may have been needed.

I was so busy that I did not check the order until I started the job. I looked in the box, and where there were supposed to be four angels, there were only two. I was so upset that I jumped into my minivan, and I noticed that the license plate on the front of my truck had fallen off; I tossed it onto the dashboard and drove off. I was on my cell phone complaining to the appliqué company about how they messed up my order when the sounds of sirens started blaring behind me.

Five tickets. One for ladders on the top of my truck on a parkway, one for an expired inspection, one for talking on my cell phone while driving (at that time, Bluetooth in cars did not exist), one for the license plate being off the truck, and finally, one for failing to wear my seatbelt. I could not hold back my hysterics—every dollar I would make from this job would now go toward paying for these tickets.

I make it a point to tell my widows to check the inspections and registrations on their cars. Now, the registrations come in the mail. Most men take care of these things, and women like me forget to look. I saved many women from going through this same brutal ordeal. Wall calendars and cell phone reminders come in handy. After those tickets, I always wear my seatbelt.

CHAPTER 10

Learning to Live— and Love—Again

Scott and our other widowed friend had heard about a "Parents without Partners" dance. The weekends were lonely, and it sounded like it might be nice, so I agreed to go. We walked into the party, and it's safe to say that we were about twenty years younger than most. The men had big bellies, covered by a loosely half-buttoned shirt, exposing curly gray chest hairs (the only hair left on their bodies besides an unkept toupée). Some of them even had hearing aids. The women were also outdated— short skirts over sagging knees, push-up bras, false lashes, and too much makeup, emphasizing, not covering, their wrinkly faces. We were like a flapping, forty-year-old fish out of water. Now that I am over sixty, my perspective is totally different.

We found a table and sat down; an older man came over right away, extending his hand toward me for a dance. To be kind, I graciously accepted and left my two male friends sitting at the table alone.

The dance was awkward, to say the least. The music was extremely loud, and we literally did not say a single word—there was no verbal communication whatsoever. I was dancing with a stranger, old enough to be my father, and all I could remember thinking was, *Whose life am I in?* When the song was over, I thanked him and sat down. It was also my first time dancing with a different man.

Scott and our other friend had gotten themselves drinks. I was engaged in a conversation with our friend about our teenagers. Scott's children were much younger, and he couldn't relate. It wasn't long before he appeared to be getting a bit jealous. Interrupting our conversation, he asked me to dance.

"Sure," I told him, and we danced.

Larry and I loved to dance, and we had our own way like I think most couples do. We met in a bar, back in the day. I recall that the first time our eyes met, it was as if an angel had spread love dust over my head because I was totally infatuated with his beautiful blue eyes and his deep auburn hair. Although I was happy to dance with Scott, it felt awfully strange, and it made me miss Larry even more.

I was pretending to have a good time, and just as quickly as my thoughts of Larry started to flood my brain, I wanted to go home.

With that, we left, and I swore I would never go back to one of those types of get-togethers again.

At that time, events for younger men and women didn't exist in many areas; it is still like this in some places. This is so much of the reason why I feel social gatherings for young widows and widowers are important. We provide this after bereavement with our groups.

Option B in My Social Life

Ella and I went to a bar one night, and immediately, I noticed how young the crowd was. I mean, they were incredibly younger than the crowd Scott and I had "mingled" with the other night, and they were noticeably younger than me and my married friend beside me. She just thought it would be good for me to get out.

She left me to use the restroom, and I was approached by a short-built, stocky, muscle man in a tight, white tee shirt baring his tattoo-covered arms. I had to be at least ten years older than him.

"So, where are your tattoos?" he asked, and I couldn't help but think, *I'm way too old for this. I don't have a tattoo.* I laughed to myself and thought, *Do stretch marks count?* but instead, I said, "I don't have one." My next thought was, *I hate my life.*

Ella returned from the restroom, and I informed her I was ready to leave. In the car, I told her about my tattoos, thoughts, and "stretch marks," and she started laughing hysterically. The whole way home, we were coming up with more lines and laughing over what his reaction would be, my favorite being the face he would make if he ever saw what my stomach looked like after giving birth three times. He'd be scared as hell!

There was basically nothing for widows and widowers as young as us. All my friends were happily married; no one was even divorced. I had no single friends. Except, there were two: Scott and our "other friend" from our bereavement group, who, if you haven't realized by now, shall remain nameless.

Thirteen Months after Losing Larry

Since he lived in the next town over, Scott and I would often drive together to and from our Wednesday night dinners. One night, we started talking about dating. I already hit my one-year mark, and he was curious about how I felt now that more time had passed.

"Nope, not for me." I didn't even need to think about it. I hated being so alone, but I absolutely could not see myself going on a dating site or something like that. Larry was my one and only.

"If I were ever to date someone, it would have to be someone like you," I said to him. I felt like Scott understood my loss. He once shared with me that he cried after his first date, and that's exactly how I saw myself reacting if I were to go on one.

"You would date me?" He misunderstood me.

"Someone like you. I didn't mean you." I panicked and repeated "not you" a couple of times before I started to feel bad. Then he said the nicest thing any man could have ever said.

"If you would date me, I won't date anyone else. I will wait for you as long as it takes."

I said," It may take me years."

He said, "I will wait if it takes you two years; I will stop dating as of tonight, "

I was stunned, and I remember questioning where this conversation was going and how did it get here. I looked at him and said, "I cannot ask you or anyone else to wait for me; I don't know if I could ever date." I left him with those word and said goodnight. I walked into my dark, empty house. My children spent the night at their friends' houses. I felt so alone.

It's a House, Not a Home

In this house, Larry died. This house was our dream house that we turned into our home and now, even my children avoided being there. I remember walking around from room to room, turning on closed lights to shine upon photos filled with memories of a life I no longer had. It was all just so overwhelmingly sad.

Our house no longer felt like a home. It was just a house. The lingering aromas from cooking our family meals were gone and replaced by the stale smell of fast food and pizza. It was silent now where boisterous laughter once echoed; the laughter left with Larry.

Larry was my home.

The day before he died, Larry and I were at the doctor's office. He was complaining that he had pain in his armpit, so the technician gave him a sonogram. The technician said, "You were here exactly a year ago by one day." It was January 15, 1999.

Larry had experienced an episode in the shower where he screamed for me that he was going to pass out. I ran, and he was white as a ghost. He said, "I felt like I was going to die. Not pass out but die."

The specialist who took the sonogram the previous year had found nothing. The doctor said he thought Larry might have had a small blood clot that had passed through, and it was not healthy for me to sleep on his right side because Larry had an unusual birth condition in his right hand and arm. For eighteen years, we'd slept in a cuddle, and now I was forced to move to my side of the bed. I was weaning all that year, always throwing a leg on him so we could still touch.

Every time I opened the door to our bedroom, I re-lived the day I opened it to see Larry dead on the bedroom floor. Every time I opened the door to the bedroom I once loved,

I was triggered, and the visual memory of the day he died was activated.

◇◇◇

Back in my bedroom, to distract myself from the memories of the day Larry died, I started to think of the conversation Scott and I shared in the car. It was how I was surviving the trauma by switching my thoughts frequently from death to the present moment. What Scott said was really the sweetest thing anyone had ever said to me, and as I was falling asleep, I was wondering if Larry would have waited to date me two years like Scott.

That night, I dreamt of Sally.

I didn't even know what she looked like, but I knew it was her, and she was beautiful. She looked like an angel, and we were talking, but not with words. Telepathically. She communicated with me through love, and she made me feel a sense of acceptance. It was the strangest dream, and I was too embarrassed to share it with anyone, so I kept it to myself for a long, long time. I later read in many near-death experience stories that when a person dies, and they meet others, they communicate telepathically.

They also share these intense feelings of love.

I believe Sally and I love her children together. I often include her in my prayers.

◇◇◇

That week was another long and lonely week, with every thought being about Larry; I couldn't believe how surreal all of this was. I occasionally joke to my groups how I thought of Larry more after he died than when he was here!

Larry and Me

It was like I could not think of anything else without going back to thoughts of him. I know; only someone who experienced this would know exactly what I mean.

In the End, We Only Regret the Chances We Didn't Take

It had been two weeks since Scott told me he would wait for me, and it was my second lonely weekend in my house. Every day felt like Groundhog Day. My friends were out with their husbands, my children were out with their friends, and I was alone again. I had the realization that Larry was truly never coming back, so I picked myself up from the couch, turned on the computer, and sent an email to Scott.

This was the night I realized that if I didn't change something, nothing else would. In an email, I wrote, "I have decided to have a cup of coffee with you." It was just coffee, I thought to myself; I wasn't going to marry him.

Dating after twenty-three years of being only with Larry was extremely difficult. What helped was that Scott and I were already friends; it kept us from having an awkward stage. I never saw myself dating anyone else. Why would I?

We never know what the future holds for us.

Just the way one person loved you, someone else one day can. I realize now that it was up to me to keep this door open for opportunity.

Scott and I started emailing each other more frequently when we could not be together. He was dating, and so was the other guy from our group; I was convinced, however, that I would never date again or remarry. I was dealing with tons of legal stuff from Larry's estate, and both Scott and I had medical negligence suits pending.

When Sally passed, Scott's children were four, six, and eleven; mine were eleven, fourteen, and eighteen. Scott and I were the same age, born two weeks apart, and Sally and Larry were also the same age, born two weeks apart. We both had two sons and a daughter (both of our daughters were the youngest of our lot); we both ran in the same races, and we had one acquaintance from the local Y who knew us with our spouses. She declared that she could not see us together, but then again, at first, neither could I.

Trust Your Intuition

In the first few months following Larry's passing, I decided to install a more sophisticated alarm system around my house to help me feel more secure.

It just so happened that while the men were there to install the system, my doorbell rang, and I opened it to see a worker Larry had hired to install our pond from the previous summer.

My intuition told me he was trouble from the start. I always felt like he was undressing me with his eyes, and I told Larry that I did not care for this worker nor the way he looked at me; Larry assured me that I had nothing to be concerned about and that all the dealings would be conducted through him. I remember Larry counting the last of the money he owed this man, remarking that he was paying him in full. Why would he be here now, months later?

"Can I help you?" I kept my right hand firmly grasped upon the doorknob and my right foot behind the door, not allowing him to come in.

"I don't know how to ask you this, but Larry owes me a thousand dollars for the pond I installed; he never had the chance to pay me."

I couldn't believe this guy—he was looking for a handout from a job that happened six months prior to Larry's dying. Here he was lying to me. a woman who just lost her husband.

"My husband paid you in full months ago, and I was there to see it!" I slammed the door in his face, and I remember being grateful that he came just as the men from the alarm company exited my home after installing my new system. He never bothered me again.

It is not uncommon for widows to be taken advantage of financially.

Dating sites are also notorious for this, and I make it a point to educate widows about the "red flags" they may face. Men have been known to stage their profiles, adorned with uniforms, pets, and God-fearing messages, appearing to be kind and well-intentioned, which is why it's so important to be hyper-vigilant. I have heard horror stories—one woman dated a man for a year who continually borrowed small amounts of money that he could reasonably pay back. When he asked her for a larger sum, he bailed with all her mortgage money.

A widow should never lend money to anyone. Sadly, I also know of a woman whose son robbed her of the life insurance policy she inherited, insisting on a get-rich-quick business he had.

We must take care not to trust everyone when it comes to money. We are vulnerable, and it's as if the scammers can smell us from miles away. This is where my Brooklyn comes in. Never ever give money out; you just say, "I don't know what my future holds."

I learned recently of another scam where, after some time in the relationship, the boyfriend asks for nude photos and then tries to blackmail the person by threatening to show their children or people at work. Just be on your guard: if it feels wrong, walk away.

◇◇◇

After Larry died, I could no longer afford the same luxuries, and it was only a matter of time before I would not be able to afford our home.

I had to tell my cleaning man, Jose, that I couldn't afford his services much longer, and after cutting him from every week to every other week, I soon had to let him go altogether. During one of his last visits to the house, I needed him to look at the toilet in our guest bathroom. It hadn't been working properly, and I felt like everything in the house was breaking. I hated not knowing how to fix anything; he wanted to help me and told me he could fix the toilet. I needed to get a flagger. If I went to Home Depot to get a new one, he would gladly fix it for me.

Grateful, I rushed to Home Depot and made a beeline for the plumbing aisle to find a flagger. I must have gone up and down the same aisle three times before a salesman noticed me awkwardly looking around and asked me if he could help. Relieved, I told him I was looking for a flagger, to which he replied, "What's a flagger?" After describing what looks like a rubber thing that goes in the tank on the back of the toilet, he bursts out laughing and says, "You mean a flapper!"

Jose, born and raised in Nicaragua, had a very thick Spanish accent, and I must have misunderstood him. In the car, I laughed alone. Larry would have thought this was very funny, and I missed the intimate banter we used to have; I knew he would have had a few things to say about this one, and I desperately wished he was there to say it.

Repairs are another thing that can overwhelm us in our widowhood. Asking our neighbors or other family members for help can sometimes feel like an imposition—even if they claim it isn't.

We cannot do it all alone.

I have created a separate Facebook Networking page for our groups just for this purpose. In this group, if someone is looking for a handyman, electrician, painter, etc., we share who we trust in our homes and recommend them to each other. I make it my business to try to know all my members. We truly try our best to help each other.

◇◇◇

Scott asked me to help him paint and decorate his house; when I went to look at the rooms, I met his children.

Jordana was the most beautiful little girl. Zach was also adorable, and Brett and I had already known each other from the bereavement group that Danielle and Anthony had previously attended. They had just brought home a Siamese kitten, and they were all gushing over it when I arrived.

Before Scott and I were married, I had to go to therapy for my fear of cats. My sister often joked with me about my marrying Scott: "You really must be blonde, marrying a man with three children."

"It's not the kids I'm worried about," I joked back. "It's the cat!"

In the end, I was okay with the cat. He was smart, and he never jumped up on me.

◇◇◇

One day, when visiting Scott, Jordana's beautiful green eyes were all red and swollen. I asked him what had happened, and he told me that some of the girls at school refused to play with her because her mommy died. This beautiful little girl was being bullied because her mother was dead. I encouraged Scott to call the school and speak with the principal before it got out of control.

Children bullying children who have lost a parent is not unheard of, but it is incredibly difficult to accept. If you have children in school, it is so important to speak with your child's teacher and to make sure that they are aware of your situation at home as well as in their classrooms. I have heard from far too many members over the years who have encountered this same problem. Some parents won't allow their children to attend a home where a mother is not present. For the child, it is so important for them to just blend in with the other kids. Some children do not want the teachers to know they lost a parent.

◇◇◇

When I went back to paint some of the rooms in Scott's home, he was often at work. It was early in the morning that I would arrive, so I was able to observe his children independently getting ready for school. One morning, Zachary, who was only seven or eight at the time, was funneling jellybeans into his mouth—it was 8:00 a.m.

"Jellybeans, Zach?" I looked at him with surprise.

"Daddy lets me eat jellybeans in the morning as long as I eat all of my breakfast."

When I spoke with Scott later that day, I asked him why he allowed that, and as quickly as the question left my lips, he was adamantly denying it. We laughed and laughed. Now, I had Zach's number—he could look me straight in the eye and tell a fib. This was quickly corrected.

Solo Parenting

Sleeping at night was incredibly difficult. One evening, I had to use the bathroom, and from outside the window, I could see flashing lights in my yard. A group of teens were having a bonfire in the woods outside of my house . I freaked! I grabbed my robe and flew down the steps, opened my backdoor, and screamed for my son Michael, who ever so nonchalantly walked toward me from his makeshift fire pit and said, "Hey, Mamma. What's up?"

"What's up?" I screamed, "There is a fire in my yard!"

"Mom, chill," he said, "it is in a tire; everything is safe."

I started hyperventilating. "Michael, put it out now, or I will call the police!"

He looked at me like he had never seen my face before. "Sure, Mom, I'll put it out, but I am telling you, it's safe." I assured him that I didn't care what he thought, and with clenched teeth, I told him again to put the fire out.

I could not believe I was doing this without Larry. How was I going to raise teenage boys without him? I mean, who has a fire in the middle of the woods?

That same week, Michael tattooed "La Famiglia" in large letters across his back; it looked like a billboard for the Sopranos. On his ankle, he tattooed his father's initials. He didn't ask my permission to do this; he just went ahead and did it.

On another occasion, Michael had to have his tonsils removed. Three weeks following the surgery, the doctor confirmed that he was healing properly, but he still needed rest and more recovery time before going back to work.

In the early hours of the morning, my son decided it was a good time to do some pushups. He hadn't been able to work out since his surgery, for obvious reasons, yet he figured there was no harm in a little over-exertion.

It was three o'clock in the morning on the Fourth of July weekend, and running into my room comes Michael, hemorrhaging from his mouth. He popped his stitches, and for the second time that year, I had to rush to the emergency room; the first time was when they pronounced my Larry dead.

My mother came to my house to stay with Anthony and Danielle while I stayed at the hospital with Michael; he hemorrhaged for next four hours until the doctor cauterized his throat.

Sure, if Larry were still around, I would still have been scared, but it was the support—the partnership—of being in these things together that I needed and missed the most.

I felt like I was losing total control of my children. I couldn't handle the grief; I was totally miserable, and it was so difficult to find the strength to handle my own children.

Each night, before going to bed, I would visit each of my children and give them a kiss goodnight. One night, I noticed that Anthony's hand was wrapped in gauze. The following morning, when I asked him what had happened to his hand, he casually replied that he banged it on something.

I later found out that Anthony had ripped the skin off his knuckles one night while pummeling the punching bag in our basement. My neighbor took care of him, and I was so grateful for her help, but I couldn't help but feel sad, hurt, and guilty that my children were no longer coming to me for help. I could only assume that Anthony didn't want to cause me to worry or cause me any more pain than he saw I was already going through.

As scary as all these experiences were, I did get through them. Of course, I didn't choose to have to go through these things alone, but never in a million years did I think I would have been able to endure half of the things I faced. I say frequently in groups: we are so much stronger than we think we are.

Widows are not single parents; we are "solo" parents, and we are missing a lot more than just a second income and shared custody. We don't have anyone to share the decisions in raising them. Many of the children like mine have been traumatized as well, missing the parent that passed. Some of the kids are very angry and some hide their emotions.

What Would Larry Do?

Larry and I were so in tune with each other, especially with each other's facial expressions. I always say that if we were at a party together but, for whatever reason, we were standing on opposite sides of a room, someone could walk between us, and we would be able to look at each other and know exactly what the other was thinking. We would laugh and laugh at how often we would finish each other's sentences. It was this connection that helped me raise my children, even after he was gone.

Knowing what Larry would have wanted without having to discuss it was something I counted on. I would ask myself, "What would Larry do?" and then I'd laugh because, let's face it, I didn't listen to everything he would say, in life or in death!

Michael was dating a girl from New Jersey, and he asked if she could sleep over. I immediately thought that Larry would never allow her to sleep in the same room; after all, we have two younger children at home, and I wouldn't want to give them the wrong message. We agreed that she could sleep on the extremely large and comfortable sectional in the den, but at 5:30 the next morning, upon getting up to go to the gym before work, I noticed that there was no sleeping beauty on my sofa.

I decided to prepare myself a cup of coffee and put away the pots and pans from last night's dinner, and every thought started rushing through my head. Maybe she just fell asleep in his bed, or maybe Michael just flat-out refused to follow my very clear instructions. I started banging the pots and pans before putting them away in hopes that they would both wake up and she would come running out of his room. However, this didn't work.

I continued drinking my coffee, and the thought popped up, *What would Larry do?* He would go right into Michael's room without hesitation, but I couldn't help but hesitate a little; I was not prepared for what I might be walking into. I decided banging on the door was the next best option.

"WHAT?!" Michael screamed from behind his door.

I opened it. "Where is she?!" I demanded.

"She's on the couch!" he responded.

"I looked on the couch!" I spoke sternly.

"The other one!" he replied.

"Good!" I said, embarrassed, and closed his door.

I didn't think to look in my living room. Instead of stretching out on our large sectional, Michael had set her up on a tiny loveseat, and though I didn't understand this choice, I felt embarrassed that I hadn't looked. When I got back from the gym, they were both dressed nicely and preparing to leave for work. As I hugged Michael goodbye, I whispered in his ear, asking if everything was okay.

"Yeah," he said, "she just mentioned that you are loud when you put your pots away."

I smiled and held back a laugh, and they left.

CHAPTER 11

The Five-Year Prayer

After a year had passed since losing my Larry, I was made aware of the five stages of grief as they were coined by a Swiss-American psychiatrist named Elizabeth Kubler-Ross in 1969. According to her, getting through grief starts with denial, then anger, then bargaining, then depression, and finally, acceptance. Now, as I said, it had been a year, and many of these stages simply did not feel accurate to me, but who am I to argue with therapists and their theories? I was just living it every day and speaking daily with two friends living through it, as well.

I decided to do some self-evaluation and determine what I may have been missing:

Denial: I was not in denial about Larry's death; we were never separated. I was very much aware that he was not in my bed every night, and he never would have left me for that long of a time.

Anger: I was angry; yes, this was true, but I was angry that I could not control what had happened or what was currently happening. None of my anger was directed at Larry; if he'd had a choice, I know he would have stayed. I was angry at the doctor for the misdiagnosis, but I was not consumed with this emotion.

Bargaining: I had no reason to bargain. Bargain for what? He was already dead. What deal could I possibly make?

Depression: I was not depressed in the way many people are who battle mental illness, but I was certainly overwhelmingly sad.

Acceptance: Never, in twenty-three years, have I felt a sense of acceptance over Larry's death. To me, acceptance meant that I was okay with what happened, and that has never occurred. What I did accept, however, was moving forward with my life.

Navigating the "Five Stages" of Grief

My confidence in myself was faltering by the minute, and I was overwhelmed with fear. Hell, according to these five stages, I couldn't even grieve properly!

People kept implying they recognized what stage I was in, only frustrating me more. I felt like I had twenty stages of grief from my loss—lack of confidence, anxiety, fear, worry, being overwhelmed, and exhaustion were only a few, not to mention that I felt like I was a horrible mother to our children. I took naps every chance I could get because I was physically and emotionally exhausted from crying, leaving my children to essentially support our household.

I even had to push myself to go to the gym, something I always loved doing and something that had become essential in alleviating at least some of my stress. As time continued to pass, this was becoming more of a deep-seated reality, a reality I totally hated.

I was struggling with this "new normal." My children had always been my everything, and this pain was separating me from those I loved most. On one particular day, I remember looking through the clothes hanging in my closet and realizing I didn't even like them. *Why am I wearing them?* I thought to myself. *Did I wear them for Larry?* I started to question everything. "Who am I?" was the question plaguing me.

I believe this is one of the biggest secondary losses we feel in widowhood; this stage should be called, "Who am I *now?*"

Losing your partner differs from all other types of loss because of this loss of identity. We do everything with our partners—I even wore my hair and dressed a certain way for Larry because I knew he liked it. We plan our future according to how we envision it together. When I lost Larry, I lost myself, and I felt like I had no idea who I was anymore.

Kubler-Ross's book about the five stages of grief was meant to be read by those who were losing their own lives, not by those grieving the loss of someone else's. Apparently, many people, grievers, and therapists alike, confuse the purpose of this book, causing the grief itself to be all the more confusing.

Only five stages? What about all the secondary losses that we feel? I have discovered that many people are simply winging it through grief, and being told that there are specific stages to get through makes everything even more puzzling, not to mention overwhelming.

Neuroscientist Mary O'Connor Frances wrote in her book, *The Grieving Brain*, that the five stages are a model for the description of grief, not a prescription on how to grieve.[4] When we think everyone is supposed to go through it this way, it becomes damaging.

Sometimes, people just need to feel what they are feeling without rules or stages—both of which can be limiting, causing even more challenges. We all just need someone to be there for us. My self-esteem took a nosedive after losing my biggest fan, and I've learned that this is a common struggle endured by many grieving widows and widowers. My self-esteem was attached to my husband's love because he saved me from my abandonment issues from my dad.

◇◇◇

To sleep, I took all the pillows from our bed and placed them on the side where I used to sleep before Larry died. I chose to sleep on his side—one glance at his empty place in our bed was a reminder that he was gone, and I couldn't bear it. When I slept on his side of the bed, I didn't wake up to an immediate storm of sadness, and though I hated sleeping alone, I could sleep.

The pillow ritual was a little daunting, so sometimes I would purposely make myself so tired that I would fall asleep in my

---

4. O'Connor, Mary-Frances. *The Grieving Brain: The surprising science of how we learn from love and loss.* New York, NY: HarperOne, an imprint of HarperCollins Publishers, 2023. Page 73.

clothes on top of the covers. Missing him the way I did, with every fiber of my being, made all the small tasks feel like the most draining. Every day was physically and mentally draining.

Sometimes, on the weekends, I would allow my daughter to sleep with me. We would watch a TV show together or something of the sort. One night, I was speaking with Scott on the phone, and he fell asleep. I could hear him snoring, but before I hung up on him, I let Danielle have a listen so we could share a giggle. Scott falling asleep and my experience with my first therapist who closed her eyes; I was glad I hadn't formed a complex.

When I spoke with Scott the next day, he apologized and said the antidepressants he was taking were making him sleepy. I didn't take anything for my anxiety or sadness. It caused me more anxiety to have a lack of control over my thoughts, and I did not want to compromise my children's needs; my cognitive skills had already taken a hit from my trauma and loss. I held no judgment toward Scott nor anyone for being on antidepressants—I understand all too well that losing the love of your life can cause the saddest emotions. They just weren't for me.

Life's Picture Is Constantly Undergoing Change

I was encouraged by my neighbor, Jane, to sue the physician who misdiagnosed Larry's condition. Jane was a lawyer, and after some time had passed since the initial filing, I stopped by her home to say hello.

We spent most of the morning talking, but Jane had to go to Riverhead on some legal business that afternoon. She asked me if I wanted to join, so I took the ride with her. In the car, we discussed my case. The partners at the law firm I filed my case with had separated—one moved to the city and the other to Long Island—so I had very little idea about what was happening, but I assumed one of them was working on it, and no one had contacted me. She told me when we got there that she was going to investigate it to see where it was. I didn't even know that she could do this. She found my lawsuit in an inactive file. Neither lawyer had taken it.

The statute of limitation on a medical negligence lawsuit at that time was nine months after a loss, it had been eight and half months since Larry's passing. Whatever prompted me to join Jane on her ride to Riverhead essentially saved my lawsuit. The steps and events that happened, and the timing, seemed so synchronous; I always thought it strange that I just so happened to stop over at Jane's house on the same day she was making that trip. I thought it was even stranger that I had decided to go with her. The laws on this have changed, and, as of right now, you have two years to file a suit. I always feel that some of the synchronicities that occur after loss seem more like we are being helped from the other side.

When we came back from Riverhead, Jane called my lawyer herself, and for the second time, I had to meet with him to review every single detail about what had happened to Larry. Thankfully, I wrote everything that happened down in the beginning, as being in the state I was in at that time, there was no way I could have remembered everything or anything the same way. He admitted that it could take up to five years for the lawsuit to resolve. I felt like my life was a never-ending nightmare. Knowing the suit could take up to five years, I came up with a five-year plan and recited this prayer every night before laying my head down to sleep.

Lord, please give me five years, five years till my children are grown, and then please take me too.

Boundaries

It was President's week in February, and Scott reminded me about the trip he had planned the prior year to take his kids to Florida. This was the same trip that his ex-girlfriend had unexpectedly booked to join him. This was the same ex-girlfriend to whom he could never say no, the one I nicknamed Gum-on-Your-Shoe, and she was still planning on crashing their vacation. He missed my birthday while on vacation that year. I remember he called to wish me a happy one in the same sentence that he was telling me about the dinner he'd just had with Gum. I was furious and hung up on him. Scott and I had only had one date, but I was feeling insecure about this woman.

He called later in the week and told me he wasn't sleeping with her. They had separate rooms, and he assured me that they were just friends. He said he simply didn't want to lie to me about where he was, and I tried to appreciate his honesty; if he had never told me, I suppose I never would have known.

The problem was that this woman was calling him all the time, and though Scott kept insisting they were only friends, she became an annoyance. Maybe I'm out of the loop, but who sleeps with someone and then just becomes "friends" with that same person? Nonetheless, she always called on a Saturday evening when we would be out. Scott would pick up the phone, and I would sit silently in the passenger seat, listening to their entire conversation.

I had been with Larry for so long that being in this new role was extremely confusing. I had no idea how to act, and I absolutely did not want Scott to see exactly how insecure I was feeling. I tried desperately to behave like nothing bothered me, but the truth was it was making me feel like I wasn't a priority.

Every weekend, Scott would ask me to join him on his boat with his children, but my weekends were still so busy with doing work estimates and laundry for the week. One weekend, I decided I was going to surprise him. I packed up some sandwiches, got in the car, and when I was five minutes away, I called him.

"Surprise!" I said, "I'm coming to meet you on the boat!"

He was in the bay when I called, on a dinghy with some friends, and it turned out that the surprise was on me. "Gum-on-Your-Shoe is here; I invited her."

I could feel the Brooklyn tomboy in me coming through— the one who is never scared of a good fight—and I remember thinking, *Look out, Gum.*

Screw this girl! Scott and I were dating now, and I had a right to be there.

Being that girl from Brooklyn, I had no idea how to dress for boating. I showed up wearing dress pants, high wedge shoes, big earrings, and red lipstick—not your proper everyday boating attire. When I arrived, I saw Zach, Scott's son, sitting on a woman's lap, whom I assumed to be her; they were sitting in a circle of people. I walked right up to the boat and screamed, "Hi Zach!" forcing a huge smile with my cherry-colored lips and waved.

They all are staring at me, watching me walk onto the boat with my high heels and big loop earrings, their mouths wide open, looking shocked.

I wonder, now that I do know how to dress, if they were just surprised, as Scott was surprised, by my impromptu visit or if it was the way I was improperly dressed for boating that caused them their amazement; nevertheless, all mouths were open—even seven-year-old Zach's.

When I got on the boat, I walked to the galley to put the sandwiches away, and Gum followed me. She introduced herself, and I extended my hand to shake hers, but she threw my hand up in the air.

Kindly, I said, "Would you like a sandwich," firmly implying that it was my place to be there, not hers.

"I think it's time for me to leave," she said.

I replied, "Yes, I agree."

I knew that ticked her off, and I thought to myself, *I fight nicely now that I'm all grown up.*

When I saw Scott, he looked incredibly nervous, but I acted like nothing had happened. We enjoyed the day together, and it wasn't until that evening, after putting his children to bed, that

I told him exactly how I felt. "I was used to being married to a man who adored me and me only. I don't know how to feel about this Gum you constantly have stuck to the bottom of your shoe! She never goes away!"

He looked at me, laughed, and said, "She's just a friend," but this friend thing was not working for me.

"Sorry," I said, "but I'm out. I'm not comfortable with how this friendship is making me feel, and I'm not going to move forward in a relationship with you while this woman lurks in every corner."

He was shocked, but he immediately declared that our relationship meant more to him than this friendship, and to my relief, he ended it that night.

◇◇◇

We are so vulnerable after loss, and I think the thought of being alone could have compromised my decision to speak up, but I needed to be true to myself. It wasn't until later that I found out that when they arrived in Florida, Gum's credit card was declined, so she assumed she would have to stay in Scott's room with him. He paid for her to have her own room instead, and though she promised to pay him back, she never did.

I think women have intuition about other women, and I knew she was trying to win him over the whole time. Only Scott thought they were in some weird friendship, but what really bothered me the most was that she was using his children to get closer to him by giving them gifts. She was the one who got the kitten for them.

◇◇◇

We were still meeting on Wednesdays with our other widower friend, and when we told him we were dating, he no longer wanted anything to do with us. He stopped returning our calls, he wouldn't respond to our emails, and we basically never saw him again. Back then, they didn't call it ghosting, but that was exactly what he did. We were both extremely hurt by his ending our friendship, shocked that he wasn't happy for us, and never understood why.

Dating When You Have Children

After about four months of dating, I took Danielle to visit with Scott and his children. She got along nicely with them, but none of my children were happy about the situation, especially my eldest, Michael.

Every weekend, we had the same argument; even Danielle was giving me a hard time, and they were beginning to make me feel like I was betraying Larry in some way. Eventually, I gave in, and I told Scott I could not see him anymore, an incredibly painful decision I felt I needed to make. I missed our friendship the most; he was the only person who understood what I was going through—but I never wanted my children to feel like they were not my priority. I felt that losing Larry had already separated us enough.

Intense sadness overcame me, and I stayed in bed the whole week. Breaking up with Scott compounded my grief, and it took me back to what felt like I had lost Larry again. I was desperately yearning for Larry and my old life, not wanting to worry about another relationship and not knowing what was next for me. I was not good at coping with loss. Both of my widowed friends were now estranged from me, and I had no support.

I felt so utterly lost and alone.

When new relationships or when dating does not work out, it is not uncommon to feel as though we have been thrown back into the depths of our grief. I probably dated Scott too soon, but there were no group connections or social gatherings for widows to meet widows at the time, and Scott was my best friend and the only one I felt understood me. Before I knew it, he was not only my bereavement support, but he was also my boyfriend. I said too soon because I was still crying over Larry and missing him terribly. Scott would take me away from what I was feeling, so I think it was an avoidance of dealing with what life had given me. I am not quite sure I ever met with the autonomy needed to be completely on my own.

Many people date sooner, but I knew mentally I was still missing my Larry. I didn't think in some ways it was fair to Scott, like he got half of me and Larry had all of me. I always say that Scott married a different woman than Larry. There was an innocence about me that I lost with Larry's death and the things that I went through.

When it comes to knowing whether you are ready to date, my suggestion is to ask yourself how you will handle rejection or something that doesn't work out. If it will destroy you, then maybe you're not ready. Take time to become more independent.

It's also important to consider that, when young children are involved, they become attached to whomever you are dating, and if the relationship doesn't succeed, this could develop into another form of abandonment for your children. If you are introducing your children to someone, be sure you are serious about this person and that he or she is serious about you.

Scott introduced his children to the few women he dated before me, and they all became involved—something he later realized was not good for them.

I started to notice that Michael kept checking in on me and noticing that I was struggling to push myself out of bed. He kept asking me what was wrong, but I would just tell him, "Nothing." My other two were caught up in typical young teenager stuff—too caught up to even notice anything outside of their own friendships, and I was starting to feel like I had nothing to get up for and no one to care for me! I felt that my children were self-sufficient, and my days consisted of a pity party for one.

Michael's guilt eventually caught up with him, and it wasn't long before he reached out to Scott in an attempt to have him take me back. Scott explained that he was not the one who ended the relationship, and Michael admitted that it was he who should be blamed. He explained that he just wanted his mother to be with his father, and after Scott convinced him that he was hardly trying to replace Larry, Michael drove me to Scott's house, where we eventually went back to dating.

We continued our tradition of meeting weekly on Wednesday nights. The rest of the week was often occupied by our children and their responsibilities. We also took Friday and Saturday nights for ourselves. On occasion, we could even meet on a Sunday with our children if I didn't have too many chores.

◇◇◇

I learned that death wasn't the only loss I had to learn to live with.

After two years of living in our house without my Larry, I decided it was time to downsize; it was impossible to afford all the upkeep, and since I refused to spend money on a real estate agent, I sold the house on my own. Scott and other friends of mine helped me to organize an open house, so I was never alone when it came time to show it. All of Larry's clothes still hung in his closet, exactly as they had been; no one would have had a clue that I was widowed.

Everyone had their opinions about what I should ask for my house, but I didn't listen to any of them. Eventually, I received an offer way above my asking price, and I was able to move to a house in the same school district for half the price and half the taxes. Keeping my children in the same school district was something very important to me. I felt all the changes were too much for them.

I packed up the entire house by myself, even all my children's rooms, because they were always busy, running out to school or to work. As I was still working full time, packing up the house alone was incredibly overwhelming, and even after two years without Larry, selling our home was a huge trigger for me.

I had formed so many attachments to the home we'd built together—we both put so much work into it, between the decorative paintings I produced in each room and the placement of Larry's things in his office. Moving any of his stuff caused me severe panic, so after a therapist recommended taking an antidepressant, I did what I was told out of desperation.

My relationship with Scott was not making moving easier; having him in my life did not make me miss Larry less. Something new does not erase something you once had, not for me, at least. I had a very difficult time separating losing my home from losing Larry. It all felt, in some strange way, like another death. I was attached to the history we had in the house we called home.

In therapy, I was asked to identify what worried me most, and through an ocean of tears, I managed to croak out the words "erasing him," and she clarified for me that just because I was moving did not mean that I had to give away his stuff. She suggested that I take them with me—such a simple solution but not one I had considered—and so when the time came to pack up his closet, I neatly folded his clothing, placed his other possessions in a box, and labeled it "Larry's Things."

After a short time on antidepressants, I started noticing some behavioral changes in myself. I started not to care about things anymore—from making my bed to leaving dishes in the sink, and my work was being neglected. This was all out of character for me. With no one to rely on but myself, I stopped taking the medication and started getting back to being me.

It was in this new house that I felt myself becoming independent, and I felt myself growing around my grief. Though moving was an incredibly difficult decision to make, it was not one I rushed into. Each decision came with careful consideration, and I am proud of myself for being certain of each choice I made before moving forward with it.

One book that helped me greatly during this time was *Who Moved My Cheese?* by Spencer Johnson, M.D., and later I read *Out of the Maze* by the same author. Both books have to do with change and how to handle it, and I highly recommend them to anyone finding themselves in situations where the inevitability of change becomes an incredibly overwhelming truth to accept.

Although I lived in our new house for only two years, I did all I could do to make it perfect for me and my kids. I took time to decorate each room and painted murals to make it uniquely our own.

I quickly learned, however, that listening to music while painting was no longer a good idea. Every love song was about Larry and me, and it caused me to become too sad. Talk radio was my station of choice—even in my car—and it would be years before I could really enjoy listening to music again.

All of this was part of my survival mode. I had to be more positive, and anything that caused me to feel otherwise would need revamping. Going to the cemetery every morning, for example, made me sad. I learned that it was okay to go only on special occasions and that visiting Larry's grave was not going to bring me closer to him.

He was always right where I needed him to be, in my heart.

CHAPTER 12

We Don't Know
What We Don't Know

It was Brett's Bar Mitzvah. This was the first real public social gathering I would be attending since losing Larry. While getting dressed to go, I began to panic to the point of no return, and I officially had what I came to understand was my first anxiety attack. All of Sally's family and friends would be there, and the more I thought about it, the more anxious I became, but the last thing I wanted to do was disappoint Scott.

I must have changed my clothes half a dozen times. I put my hair up, then down, then up again. I was a mess. Before I knew it, two hours had elapsed, and the prayer ceremony was over—I had missed it completely. The later it got, the more anxious I became. I called my sister Lisa, sobbing.

After she calmed me down, I picked myself up and went to the celebration. Scott asked me," Where were you?" but I told him I could not talk about it, and he left it at that. He told me he was happy that I was there, and he never pressured me to tell him what had happened, which was another reason to love this man. Sally's mother, their family, and friends all treated me very nicely, and while the montage of family photos circulated on the large screens situated in the party room, I found myself feeling less uncomfortable about my situation and sorrier that Scott's children were without their mother. It took the focus completely off me.

Becoming attached to Scott's children concerned me because I could not be sure where our relationship was headed. His two younger children needed to believe we were just friends, and I told them that their father was a catch, but truly, they were the icing on the cake. Zachary loved sweets, so the visual made him excited. He declared himself as the cherry on top and made me laugh out loud. I confirmed to him that he was, in fact, the cherry on top. It was so important to me that they knew how special they were. I was concerned with all the abandonment they had experienced from all the people who came in and out of their very young lives.

At the time of Brett's Bar Mitzvah, I didn't know how to regulate myself to bring myself out of a panic attack. Now, you can find one of many breathing exercises on YouTube to help you catch yourself and regulate your present situation. Personally, I like Kati Morton's channel. I believe that most who are young don't expect death to happen to their person and, therefore, become traumatized when it happens.

There is also a lot of information on the Vagus nerve, which takes a long and winding course through the body—the longest cranial nerve. This nerve is responsible for various bodily functions, including digestion, heart rate, and breathing. It is an essential part of the parasympathetic nervous system, which controls rest and digestion, and the Sympathetic Nervous System, which is responsible for calming organs after the stress of fight-or-flight response to danger.

Not to get too scientific, but just to help you understand what you might be going through, the Sympathetic Nervous System is responsible for calming organs after stress. During trauma, our bodies can hold onto fear and put us on edge, keeping us in a constant state of hypervigilance. In this position, the person is overstimulated and unable to calm themselves. They keep waiting for something else bad to happen.

Anxiety, anger, restlessness, panic, and hyperactivity can all happen. I believed my life was in a state of fear every day right after Larry died. There are trauma therapists who understand this and help calm your nervous system—muscle memory and the mind-body connection to our mental and physical experiences that feed each other. Numbness can also be a trauma response from being overwhelmed with feelings.

Trauma is stored in the physical body, so movement is helpful.

Some of the different modalities that have helped many with the anxiety that comes from the trauma are somatic therapy, EMDR Therapy, tapping, mindful meditation, exercise, yoga, going into nature, deep breathing, and playing with small children or pets. You can also wash your face with cold water or rub an ice cube on your face . The book *Unwinding Anxiety* by

Judson Brewer, MD, PhD helped me with learning mindfulness meditation. I took an eight-week course recommended in the back of the book and found it helpful.

During the COVID pandemic, I experienced anxiety attacks again, so I would just walk. The walking and fresh air calm me. There is a popular quote from C.S. Lewis in his book *A Grief Observed*: "No one ever told me that grief felt so much like fear"; it was the physical symptoms that he was feeling after the death of his wife, Joy—the inability to take in what anyone is saying, what we call brain fog or widow fog, that comes over us. It can be a duality, where we need family and friends and yet can't follow the conversation. This is what led me to my moments of isolation. That fog stayed with me for quite some time; crowds and loud noises were disturbing to me. Much was told to me that later I cannot recall.

Anxiety or panic attacks are common after grief. However, they are not the same. I was experiencing anxiety attacks. Panic attacks that are sudden, unexpected, and more intense can also happen. Just be kind to yourself; you are doing the best you can. I was accomplishing so much but always concentrating on what more I needed to do. Try to count the things you have accomplished and consider them as a win.

The Task of Bill-Paying

You don't realize all the things your partner did until their responsibilities become yours. Paying and sorting through the bills was Larry's task. I thought I paid the insurance bill. Six months later, the same exact payment was due. I called the company and complained, thinking they must not have received my check. "Lady," the man on the line said to me, "it's called a premium, and you pay it twice a year." And that was when I learned what a premium was.

I also had no idea how to use a debit card; I learned that with no credit card in my name, I had no credit. I remember going to the bank feeling ashamed that, as a grown woman, I had never learned how to do this. I was praying that no one from my neighborhood would be there to witness my incompetence. I approached the teller and asked her to explain a few things to me, and I remember feeling embarrassed that I had never been curious about how to do things like this; I was happy to let Larry take care of it all. Perhaps he knew he was better at paying bills and managing things like this. He often would share with me something financial that he was doing for us and our children, just to keep me included.

There are many widows whom I have met who are already in charge of matters like this. I tell them they are in a much better place than I was because bill paying was a huge part of my being so overwhelmed. I never had to do these things, and I had no idea where to start. I still laugh about not knowing what a premium was, but I recognize that having experience in doing this was a start in making better financial decisions. It wasn't that I could not figure out the bill paying; I just never had to. The letter of testamentary, being executrix of his estate, all this legal terminology I had never heard before. We have lawyers and financial advisers in our group who are so helpful for people who are in the position I found myself in.

Sometimes You Just Have to Laugh at Yourself

I was driving home from Brett's Bar Mitzvah alone, and I noticed that I was running out of gas, so naturally, I pulled into the gas station to fill up my car. I'd never had to pump my own gas before, but I figured it couldn't be too difficult.

I rushed out of my car and entered the little convenience store. There were a few people shopping around, but I rushed ahead of them to the line at the register and spoke to the man behind it.

Pointing toward my vehicle, I asked, "Excuse me, sir, I need to get gas, and that's my car over there." "Okay," he said, "what number?"

"Over there," I replied as I continued to point.

"All the tanks are numbered," he said. "What's the number?"

Confused, I told him to hold on, and I ran in my four-inch heels out toward the tank adjacent to my car. I found the number and ran back inside to see a rather lengthy line that had formed in front of the register. The attendant waited for me to come back.

"It's 87," I loudly proclaimed from the door, and everyone in the store started laughing. "Lady," he said, "that's the octane. The numbers are only one through four."

Puzzled by the laughter, I ran back to the tank, and I saw the number four, painted in a bright yellow on the side of the pump. This would later become an example of one of the many things I didn't know simply because I'd never had to learn.

I hated that I did not know how to do basic things. Later, I was able to laugh at myself along with the other patrons in the store and in my groups when I shared this story. I was providing validation for all of those "dumb blonde" jokes, and now I can laugh, but at that time, I was trying to survive, and these small nuances made me feel like I was lost.

Till Death Do You Part

When Scott first started telling me he loved me, I would kindly ask him to stop. I loved him as a friend, but I did not feel as if I was in love, and I was certainly not just going to say it because he said it first. After a few months, however, I found myself really looking forward to being with him, and after a year or so had elapsed, something changed.

We still had beepers at the time, so I sent him this message, which was the lyrics of an old song called "More Today Than Yesterday" by Spiral Staircase: "I don't remember what day it was; I didn't notice what time it was; all I know is that I fell in love with you." Scott, being the same age as me, knew exactly what I was sending him.

He wanted to get married, but I wanted things to stay just as they were. He gave me an ultimatum: "I can't continue to date you if you feel that there is no future for us."

I felt trapped, and I told him to let me think about it. I loved him. I was certain that I did, so what was my issue? Here I was again, forced to decide something that I felt I simply could not do. Since Larry passed away, I just lived for the day, and here Scott was asking me to think about the future. *Take it day by day*, everyone tells you, and for so long, that was exactly how I was getting by.

To be honest, thinking about the future gave me anxiety, and so I told Scott I would marry him on one condition: that when I died, I would be with Larry, and when he died, he would be with Sally. He did not hesitate to agree, and a few months later, he got me a ring.

It's a complicated situation to love again and still love your person. I would think it wouldn't have been possible if it hadn't happened to me. Larry taught me what real love is. I didn't have to stop loving him to love Scott. It was a duality. It just wasn't the future I had planned for myself. Then again, does everything we plan always go as expected?

My business was doing so well that I had practically no time at all to even think about wedding plans, much less a wedding dress. I remember when Ella called me to say that she and her son had found a wedding dress for me, and since I knew she knew me well enough, I trusted her taste, ran to the store, and bought the dress on the spot.

Scott planned everything else; we each invited fifty people, and in late September of 2004, four and a half years after Larry died, Scott and I were married.

I did not want to be without Scott. I truly loved him, and still, now, when I am with him, I can stay in the moment, just as I promised myself I would. He gets me, he accepts me, and he loves my children. I just had one more thing to do, and that was to pray to God to forget about that five-year plan I had so adamantly begged for repeatedly.

Now, I so wanted to live.

Scott's son Brett was his best man; Zach and Jordana were our entire bridal party. My son Michael walked me down the aisle, and my daughter Danielle was my maid of honor. Anthony showed up about five minutes before the ceremony and reluctantly joined. Danielle looked miserable in many of the wedding photos, and it was clear that neither she nor Anthony wanted this wedding to happen, but I felt that I had to do what was right for me. Taking on three more children was an incredibly big decision, and it was one that I had to make on my own.

The therapist I was seeing at the time assured me that my children would one day get married, leave the house, and live

Scott and I were married in 2004

Scott and me

their own lives; I too had to live mine. I had to do what I needed for me and not what my children wanted for me. She helped me to recognize the importance of not relying on anyone else's opinion but my own.

My Life, My Rules

I later learned how important it is to make certain decisions as a widow without involving your children. Discussing selling the house or selling the car with them, for example, will fuel their feelings of power over other important decisions in your life, such as who you are dating.

I had to learn to stand my ground and make my own decisions. They may mean well, but there is a fine line between what can be considered selfish and what is in your best interest. All my children have moved out, married, and started their own families. My therapist was right, and if I had ended things with Scott because my children couldn't accept him at the time, I would have never found the happiness and love I am so blessed with today. I think it's safe to say they are happy I didn't listen to them, either.

The fear of losing Scott to death, also, was something else that plagued me. Many members ask me this: I push those negative thoughts away, knowing that they come from my trauma history. What I learned about anxiety is that it is there to protect us from danger. So sometimes, we will avoid the thing we fear, but if we just go forward a little at a time, we can break the fear that the anxiety is giving us. I feel blessed to have a second chance at a second marriage.

We wanted a fresh start, and neither of us wanted to move into either of our homes, so we bought a house together. Although the house was not ready for us immediately after being married, buying a house together was the best decision we made as a blended family, and with the need for six bedrooms and a separate room for a live-in housekeeper, we quickly became known as "The Brady Bunch" to all those who knew about us and our story.

The Brady Bunch

Before we were able to move in, however, I had the ordeal of selling my second home by myself again. I was lucky to be able to sell it to the first person who saw it, and I believe that the murals and decorative painting I had done in all the rooms helped with the speediness of the sale. I was able to turn a full profit again, doing my own sale without a real estate agent, something I am proud of. Two months after being married, Scott and I finally moved into our new home.

He insisted on moving in on the same day as me, and it was absolute chaos. There were boxes everywhere—so many, in fact, that we literally could not close the door of the garage. There were a few boxes that stood out to me, however, and those were the boxes that were labeled "Larry's Things." Those boxes would come with me wherever I went until I was ready.

I was determined to remain independent and refused to give up my business. Scott's kids were still young and wished I would stop working; they were tired of being looked after by nannies, but I assured them that this time would be different. The housekeeper was a housekeeper, not a nanny, and they could come to me and Scott for everything.

Two months after the move, all our kids came down with fevers and terrible coughs. The two younger ones were sleeping with washcloths on their foreheads, and Danielle and Brett were trying to rest in their rooms. When I went to check on Brett, I caught him guzzling down the cough medicine prescribed to him by the doctor. I had never seen any of my children do something like this in the past, and it concerned me. I had to hide the medicine from him and tell him that he'd had enough, but he insisted on needing more. His behavior made me suspicious, to say the least.

The blending of our families in that first year was extremely challenging. Michael and a friend moved into a basement apartment nearby; he was twenty-two at the time, so I was okay with that. He was every bit of a young man now, and I had to respect his need for some distance. Jordana—Scott's youngest—and I, however, were locking horns. It appeared that she wanted the motherly role, but that was my role now. She was only nine years old and just as feisty as me.

What confused me most was that before I married Scott, Jordana was all over me for love and attention.

For six months, Jordana had temper tantrums; before living together, I hadn't really seen this display of behavior. I refused to let her temper tantrums overrule our new family dynamic. Danielle was starting to lose her patience and often complained about Jordana's outbursts. I knew there would be an adjustment period, and I had to remind myself that she was only four years old when Sally died and two when Sally became sick. She was just a baby. I just wanted to love her the way I loved my own, equally and without reservation.

Danielle also made it difficult for Scott; she would judge, criticize, and disrespect him at our dinner table. I had to say to her often," Do not speak to my husband that way." Thank God we all adjusted in time. I know I just had to stay consistent. Maybe it was a power play with our children, or maybe it was just a lot for children to adjust to all these changes. Just like us, they didn't ask for all this. At this time, Scott and I sought out guidance from his therapist on how to keep our family together.

◇◇◇

I remember brushing Jordana's hair one day and thinking about how unfair it was that Sally was robbed of being able to share in the joy of raising her little girl. It was so important to me that I cared for and loved Sally's children with her, and ever since I'd had that dream about her in the early days of my relationship with Scott, I felt that we had some form of agreement. She told me that she chose me, and the power of that dream, all these years later, has never faded.

After some time, I approached Scott about all the attention Jordana was getting from everyone else and how it was making my role as her stepmother (later mother) much more difficult. She had gone through a lot as a little girl, and I wanted our family to be as normal as it could be with dinners together and shared experiences. Once, when we were on vacation, and a neighbor bought her a skirt after Scott said no. The neighbor bought it for her anyway. The attention from others was not helping our family situation.

However, I felt it was different at school. It was important for me to speak with her teachers about our blended family and what this meant for Jordana. I was determined to make it clear to everyone that although Scott and I were now married, I did not and would never replace Sally—just like Scott could never and would never replace my Larry. The teachers stopped spoiling her as "the child who had no mommy," and Jordana said something to me that she was feeling like she was being ignored. I realized she was just being treated like all the other kids. I felt she still needed that extra attention. I wasn't her mommy; she still had this loss and childhood trauma. I made sure I went and spoke with each of her teachers on her behalf.

I feel very strongly about this; no one can ever replace anyone else, as no one has the same energy or spirit as another being. We are all different and unique in our own way, and each spirit with whom we are or have been connected reveals a different piece of who we are.

Danielle and Brett were spending a lot of time together. Both shared the same feelings during those "powerplay," years and with the added time they spent together on the school bus each morning and afternoon, they quickly became very close.

Zach and I were working on his tendencies to bend the truth. When I asked him about something, when it came to things like brushing his teeth, I would follow up his response with an "Okay, I'll go check," and after finding many dry tooth-brushes, he started to do what he said he was going to do. Anthony was my escaper. He really struggled with losing his father, and the blending of families was too much for him, so he was often out with friends or staying at one of their homes. It took some time, but eventually, he came around and accepted our new family dynamic.

With only fifteen months separating them in age, Zach and Jordana are remarkably close, and it was with him, especially, that Jordana assumed the motherly role. When he fell, I was the last one to know about it because she wanted to be the one to take care of him, but after observing her rushing to get ice for him one summer morning before camp, I knew some-thing bad had happened and things needed to change. He could have fractured a rib from the fall he incurred without my knowledge, and his ten-year-old sister was going to "take care of it" without telling me!

Blending a family is hard work. Scott and I agreed to speak with each other before ever responding to our children, as we wanted to make sure we

Zach at 11 and Jordana at 9

were not being played against each other. Communication is key to achieving a well-thought-out plan for raising the children and not allowing disagreements to come between you and your new relationship.

The issues with loss are not gone when we date or marry. As I've said previously, grief has no timeline. Many people assume you're over the person now that you've met someone, but there is nothing further from the truth. Our grief comes with us into every relationship, every vacation, every home. Our lost loved one is always in our thoughts.

Many years later, when my son Michael and his wife Dayna had their first child, Dayna let both her mom and me be present in the room when my first granddaughter was born. At one point, the doctor asked us to wait outside for a little bit.

While her parents embraced and shed tears of joy, my joy was mixed with sadness and a yearning for Larry. Scott did not think it necessary to go with me to the hospital as he knew all about the labor pains and how long they could possibly last. I knew, however, without a doubt, that Larry would have been there with me; nothing could have kept him away.

After the baby was born, I decided to take some time to go home for a quick change of clothes and to grab some of the many presents now stacked up in my house for this tiny new arrival. I could not wait to hold my granddaughter for the first time, so I was rushing.

I was so eager to celebrate with Scott, but as I was getting ready to go back to the hospital, he questioned me. "Why are you going back if you were just there?" I explained how I wanted to go back to hold her. He understood, but he never offered to join me. I went back to the hospital alone.

No one replaces anyone. I am blessed to have Scott in my life; however, I cannot compare or replace Larry with Scott. Scott does not have the same level of emotional excitement about things as Larry did. I know what is different, I know what to expect, and I accept that for what it is. I can't make him act or do things in the same way I knew Larry would.

Try not to compare.

∞∞

I adopted Scott's kids because I wanted us to be more united. In the years that followed, Danielle and Scott grew closer. Jordana was the Maid of Honor at Danielle's wedding, And Scott and I walked Danielle down the aisle together. He cried when she asked him. It took some time, but eventually, we all worked out to be a truly beautiful, blended family.

I know someday when Scott and I are gone, they will always have each other.

When I Realized Life Was Not What I Thought

I was painting a mural in our new kitchen one afternoon when the children arrived home from school. All of them came to see what I was doing and to say hello, but Brett made a beeline upstairs and headed straight for his room. I followed him to see what he was up to, and something seemed off to me. I thought he might have been high, but when I called Scott at work to tell him, he did not believe me.

I considered that I could have been overreacting. Brett brought a new friend home one afternoon; my suspicions grew stronger. This new friend gave me a weird feeling, and he looked like a creep. Scott explained that Brett didn't have many friends, and though I knew that to be true, I did not want this boy back in my home. I found out later that this new friend of Brett's was the same friend who had introduced him to drugs, and this was the beginning of what started to be another nightmare. Scott and I had been married less than a year at this point, and Brett was now addicted to drugs.

Brett at 16

I noticed that Danielle was not spending as much time with Brett, which comforted me now that I knew what he was starting to become involved with. I was incredibly anxious for his well-being. I started to think about my future with Scott, now with Brett, and these issues. I knew I had married him for better or worse; I just didn't think the "worse" part was going to be thought about so soon. I questioned if Scott would leave me if the roles were reversed, but I knew the answer was no, and I was determined to handle this situation just as I would have done with my own biological children.

As the years went on, Scott and I treated Brett's drug addiction together as equally loving and concerned parents. Brett's therapist explained that he was escaping from the pain of losing his mother when he was only eleven years old and from all the decisions that his father had made. Brett would often come to me to talk. I was the mediator between him and his father, and was able to get them to communicate, but I couldn't help but be completely overwhelmed and distressed by Brett's drug use. I spent countless sleepless nights, tossing and turning with fear of what his addiction meant for all of us—whether he would be robbed for drug money or worse, robbed of his life.

CHAPTER 13

Synchronicities of Life

After our one-year wedding anniversary, I decided that it was time for me to start my own bereavement group for widows and widowers who had lost their spouses at a young age. Every time I met a widow, I could fully empathize with the challenges they are dealing with. They often told me that my perspective and the way I shared my story were incredibly helpful.

I visited the place where Scott and I had met and asked the bereavement director if I could help with their groups. I was told she would have to get back to me while intimating that I was not equipped to facilitate a group on my own, primarily because I am not a social worker or psychologist. I explained that I was not looking to do this alone, but I also made it a point to tell her that living through it is more enlightening than anything that could be learned from academic coursework or a textbook.

Six weeks later, she called me and left a message on my voicemail. "We have a group for you to teach divorcees and singles how to paint!" I had no idea what she was talking about, and Scott validated my feelings of dejection when he said, "They just don't get it." He was right, and I thought I had made it clear that I was looking to help widows and widowers struggling with their loss, not for another job. With five kids at home and a full-time job, I had no interest and no time to facilitate a painting class!

∞

Meanwhile, Scott's medical negligence suit was going to court, so all his time was occupied with that, and I had to figure out what I was going to do and how I was going to start my groups without any guidance. During my despondency, I remember looking up at the wall above my desk and reading the quote I painted there: "Every great accomplishment is at first impossible."

I wasn't sure what I was going to do, but I knew I had to do something, and I was determined to get started.

I chose to start with St. Matthew Roman Catholic Church in Dix Hills, the church of our parish, and after speaking with the receptionist about my interest in starting a bereavement group, she transferred me to Sister Anthony Therese. I started to explain my intent, but before I could even finish, she exclaimed that she had just been praying and asking for help with the bereavement groups for which she was in charge. To this day, I feel strongly that this was truly a calling for me, and nothing is just a coincidence. She asked me to come to see her, and five minutes later, I was faced to face with Sister Anthony, explaining my story.

She sent me for training at the Diocese of Rockville Centre, and after completing one year of the two-year training requirement, I started my first group. We put a notice in the Sunday bulletin, and four elderly women affirmed their interest. I wanted to help younger widows like me—I knew the fears and the challenges that come with raising children alone—but I knew I had to start somewhere.

Sister Anthony and me

My group ran for a total of eight weeks. In the meantime, I reached out to other churches to let them know what I was doing, and Sister Anthony helped me make flyers to distribute at multiple funeral parlors. In all the time that she and I worked together, she kept a picture of Larry and me in her office on the corkboard that hung above her desk. She knew the depth of my pain and of my desire to do this for other men and women like me. Our picture there, in her office, was all the validation I needed to continue pushing through.

My second group consisted of twelve young widows and widowers, aged fifty-nine and younger. Susan was thirty-five, and had lost her husband, Jeff, to Lou Gehrig's disease. At home that night, I couldn't stop crying for Susan and Jeff, and I wondered if I was going to be able to do this, but I knew that I truly had no choice.

I realized quickly how important it was to separate myself from other people's grief; I could not allow anyone to pull me back to where they were. It was now my job to help them see that I was anchored in my belief and that, with the right support, they could grow the same.

I arrived at our next meeting with magazine clippings about different ways people managed difficult times in their lives, and it wasn't long before we all bonded just as I knew we would. Upon leaving one night, one of the men, Phil, stopped me and said, "You know why you're so good at this, right?" I looked at him, puzzled, as if to say no, but before I could utter any response, he said, "*Because you lived it.*"

The trauma of finding Larry had caused me to have a slow recall. Words or quick responses were a thing of the past—and this short interaction with my new group member reminded me of another interaction I had had at the gym not long after Larry died.

A young girl in her twenties approached me tenderly and said, "I heard that your husband Larry died, and I just want to express my condolences."

I thanked her for her kind words, but she continued. "My boyfriend's dog died last week, and I know how hard that was, so I kind of know how you feel."

I stared at her, unable to find any words for a reply, and I walked to the locker room. "Did she just compare her boyfriend's dog to my husband?" I was stunned, but I quickly learned that people truly don't know what to say. It comes from their ignorance about grief. We can get angry and be bitter, or we can accept that they truly don't get it; I know I didn't before I lived it.

The next bereavement group consisted of fourteen young widows and widowers, and our meetings were held on Wednesday nights. I would rush home from work, scrub the paint off me, gobble down a fast dinner, kiss Scott and the children, and rush to the supermarket for milk and cookies to accompany the free coffee donated by the church for our meetings. I always took home the leftover treats for the kids, so when I came home each Wednesday night, I was greeted with an enthusiastic "She is home!" and the tumbling of quick footsteps down the stairs.

As the years passed, I especially missed those nights, even though I knew the treats I brought home were the catalyst for all the excitement. I can still picture Brett and Zach racing each other down the stairs, laughing all the way, competing to get to me first.

About Anna

I was contacted for an interview by a woman from the Catholic newspaper. I met her at the church, and she asked me to start by telling my story. A few weeks later, a young man called regarding the article and how he felt I could help his sister. I told him that his sister would have to call me first and that it was she who had to show interest and a willingness to join a bereavement group.

Two weeks passed, and he called again, but this time, he was crying and pleading with me to make the first point of contact. His sister had recently emptied the entire contents of her home and moved her toddler, five-month-old baby, and herself into her mother's home. Her husband was forty-one and had died in his sleep. He continued to explain that her days were consumed with sleeping on the couch and leaving his mother to care for her children. I promised him I would call her but made sure he understood that there were no guarantees. I could not be certain that she would even listen to me; after all, I am a stranger.

When I called Anna, she was adamant about having lost everything, and I explained to her that I had, too.

"You don't understand," she said, "my whole life has turned upside down; I have two kids who don't have a daddy anymore."

"I do understand," I said. "My whole life was turned upside down when my husband died suddenly, leaving me with three children to raise on my own."

"I don't want to be a widow," she pleaded.

"Neither did I." I went on to explain how worried her brother was for her and that she had nothing to lose by trying out my group; she had already been through the worst, and nothing could possibly be as bad as that. After about half an hour, she agreed to join.

When we hung up the phone, I felt like I had just won an Olympic challenge. I promised her brother I would give her all I had, and I was determined to keep my word.

When Anna arrived for her first night of group, she claimed a seat without removing her coat, crossed her arms, and sat silent. I pretended not to notice the misplaced angry look on her face and treated her with kindness, but the following week, she was doing it again, and I had the feeling that when the next week arrived, she wouldn't be in attendance.

Worried, I reached out to one of the widows, Jess, from a previous group, who I knew was going to school for social work;

I felt at that time so early in helping others that I might not have the right words to convey to her the importance of connecting. I asked Jess to help me write a letter to Anna. I promised her brother I would give it all I had, and I was going to do just that.

As I was writing the letter at home, Scott walked into our office and asked me what I was doing. I explained everything to him, and his response was one of confusion.

"Why are you doing that?" he said, "Isn't this going overboard and doing more than you should have to do?"

I ignored him and figured this was where my feisty attitude came in. Just because I love Scott doesn't mean I always have to agree with him. I continued to do what my intuition was telling me to do, kept writing, and the following morning, I put it in the mail.

I received no response.

Wednesday came, and she was there. I received no response from my letter, and she made no mention of it, but there was something visibly different about her. She removed her coat, sat down, and immediately started to cry. Anna shared that she was pregnant before her husband passed away, and she felt guilty for how she treated him while dealing with her pregnancy hormones (apart from the morning sickness and lethargy, women are often challenged with mood swings during their pregnancies). We all reassured her about the normalcy of these feelings, and though her tears screamed of pain and frustration, there was a residual calm that came over her after she let herself share. I knew from this point that she was in.

She completed the whole eight weeks, and on the last night, when some of the members were hugging me and thanking me for the group, Anna walked out without a word. I was putting the final box of leftovers in my car to bring home to the kids when a white car pulled up next to me. I couldn't see who was behind the steering wheel until she rolled down her window and called out my name. "I just want to thank you, Kathryn," she said. "If you never sent that letter, I would have never come back. I am grateful that you did that."

"Thank you for trusting me with your story," I replied. We exchanged smiles and a few tender words before she drove away.

Approximately one year later, Anna wrote back to me. She explained that she was working and had met a nice man, but her overall intention for writing to me was to make it clear that it was what I said in my letter to her that caused her to get up and off her mother's couch.

It was what I said about her children that made her move; I explained that they did not want their grandmother to raise them—they still needed their mother. Their childhood was already compromised, and they needed her to try to live as though it was their lives that depended on it. I shared my own experience of being raised by my grandmother and that although I loved my grandmother dearly, she was not my mother, and it was my mother that I needed; it was my mother that I wanted. I also shared my feelings about my own children after having lost my Larry, and I admitted to thinking the same thoughts she was thinking about someone being better suited for the job, but the truth will always be that no one is better for your children than you.

My ability to read her body language enabled me to recognize her discomfort, and it reminded me of my own feelings when I was ready to quit my own group all those years ago. I quickly learned not to rely on anyone else's opinion about the way I operated my groups and trust my own intuition. The feelings of appreciation and the many transformations that I witnessed are priceless. This is what inspires me to continue. I always felt that even if I helped one person, it was all worth it.

The Lawsuits

After one hundred thousand dollars in legal fees and years of battling, Scott lost his malpractice suit. Apparently, there were certain things that could not be proven. Papers from Sally's medical chart were somehow missing. The big, fancy cancer hospital had big, fancy, cutthroat lawyers who would stop at nothing to discredit Scott, Sally, his family, and their pain.

The hospital's lawyers vilified Scott and Sally, claiming they were liars simply looking for a free ride, so Scott's attorneys urged him to bring his children to the courthouse. The younger ones were not completely aware of what was happening, but Brett was, and he was angry with Scott for not winning. Many people are never billed for legal fees on malpractice suits. Make sure you're with a lawyer who does not do this to you.

Six months later, it was my turn, and, after witnessing what Scott was going through, I was extremely nervous. The lawyer's assistant came to the house and interviewed my three children about their father. As they described Larry and the way they loved him, I could not stop myself from crying.

Danielle spoke first. "I once gave my dad a pen that was labeled with '#1 Dad.' I knew it was just a silly little pen, but my dad made me feel like it was the best thing he had ever seen. He always made me feel so special."

As she was speaking, I was reminded of the time when Larry took Danielle to the Barbizon Modeling School in New York City. For approximately eight weeks, they traveled together to and from Manhattan, where he had hoped that some of the rough and tough attitudes she was acquiring from her two brothers would be softened by the modeling experience. In retrospect, I am so happy that they had that experience together.

The boys agreed that no matter how hard their father worked or how busy he was, he never missed a single game or concert they were in. He took the whole family on vacation every year, and family time was always their favorite time. It was so hard to delve back into all these wonderful experiences with Larry and then go to bed, lying next to Scott. That night, in between twisting and turning, I had a very vivid dream about Larry. He was sitting at a banquet table, and he was making the shaking sign with his thumb and pinky, swinging his hand at me, and smiling. "So, who is your number one?" he questioned me.

I knew what he was asking, but just as I went to answer him, I was awakened by Scott's kiss goodbye. It was morning, and he was getting ready to leave for work. He told me he loved me, and I could barely mumble the words back; I just lay in bed thinking about that dream and how real it all felt. Larry looked amazing; his red hair was perfect, and his blue eyes were piercing. He looked so handsome, and he looked so happy that I could barely compose myself or will myself out of bed.

I forced myself to get up, knowing that I couldn't allow myself to go back to that painful place, and besides, I had to go to the bank. While standing in line for the next teller, I couldn't stop thinking about my dream and questioning if I was simply dreaming or if Larry was visiting me; it sure as hell felt like a real visit, but it was so hard to be sure. At that same moment, the song changed on the radio playing from the speakers above my head, and it was our song: Barry White's "My First, My Last, My Everything." My heart dropped, and I knew it was a visit, and the song was my affirmation.

As I was walking out of the bank, I received a call from a widow who was in one of my previous groups. She had a friend who had lost his wife the previous year. He was raising his three children on his own, and was struggling. She begged me to take him in, and although I was already six weeks in with the new group I was moderating, I hated to say no. I let him in.

Our next meeting would be "spiritual night," where we shared our signs and dreams, and I could not wait to share mine.

Spiritual Night

The new member's name was Larry, and he came in willingly, filled out the registration form with ease, and recorded his wife's name and how she passed away. Immediately, he started sharing with the group, and he'd had the most amazing sign from his deceased wife.

His wife loved cats, but they never had one. On the first Christmas following his wife's passing, his best friend gifted two kittens to his seven-year-old daughter: one black and white male and one ginger female kitten. Larry went on to explain that Christmas was always a huge spectacle at his home.

He would be in charge of decorating the outside while his wife decorated the inside, and while searching in the attic for ornaments that first year without his wife, his daughter found a picture frame. On it was a needlepoint picture his wife had crafted of two cats—one black and white with a blue bowtie and one ginger cat with a pink bowtie. Everyone was shocked. Even the bowties adorning the cats in the picture matched the genders of the cats they had just received in real life.

After each of the groups, I had a difficult time falling asleep. I would sit with paperwork while drinking a warm and much-needed cup of chamomile tea.

As I was sipping my tea, I opened Larry's registration sheet and flipped out when I discovered that his wife's name was Kathryn, spelled exactly like mine. "What!!!?" I screamed.

Scott asked me," What's the matter?" I threw the registration sheet up in the air.

"Larry's been communicating with me since this morning. What are the chances of having Larry and Kathryn in my group and she spells her name Kathryn exactly like mine?"

Scott said, "I wish I got signs from Sally like that."

"You probably do; you're just not picking them up." I responded. Years later, Scott was flying back from a trip to Florida and was engaged in a conversation with another passenger. They were speaking about signs. The woman told him that she receives them all the time from a loved one who passed. Scott mentioned, "So does my wife," but added that he had never received one.

She said, "They are all around us; just keep looking."

Scott told her he is just not visually aware. He said, "It would have to be hot pink for me to notice."

I had a pile of mail on our kitchen counter, awaiting Scott's return. As Scott walked toward the pile of mail. he lifted a postcard I had on top. With tears in his eyes, he said to me, " I can't believe this; I just got my first sign!" The postcard he was holding up was hot pink— addressed to Sally Douglas, who never lived at our address.

My Lawsuit

It wasn't supposed to happen.

Five years following Larry's passing and on what would have been his forty-ninth birthday, I was called into court. I wasn't allowed to have anyone come with me, and I was extremely nervous, but the fact that it was Larry's birthday gave me a sense of comfort. I can remember every detail about the walls of the courtroom and the faces of each juror as they walk in and take their seats, but the pounding of my heart deafened every other sound around me.

This went on for a few days—although it felt like an eternity—and then, on what would have been our twenty-fifth wedding anniversary, the doctor who misdiagnosed Larry walked into the courtroom.

I remember staring at him as he walked past me, and I couldn't help but think about the fact that he never apologized to me or to my children for his fatal error. The anger boiled within me, but it was prevented from spilling onto the floor when the judge called for a recess.

Spread out on a desk in the recess room were the results of Larry's sonogram. My lawyer had subpoenaed the results from the doctor's office to show proof of what I already knew was a blood clot located in Larry's armpit, which had traveled to his lungs bilaterally. As I was staring at the papers, my lawyer rushed into the recess room, asked me if I trusted him, and then urged me to settle outside of court. I did, and so we settled.

Before going back into the courtroom, I rushed myself to the bathroom for privacy, where I proceeded to cry my eyes out. I did my best to collect myself before exiting, and when I finally did, my lawyer's assistant was standing right outside. I had no doubt that he heard my sobs echoing off the bathroom tiles, but even if he could not hear anything at all, the look on my face was undoubtedly filled with anguish and screaming, all the words my voice simply could not say at the time.

After five years of life without my Larry, after five years of struggling to paint people's homes so that I could put food on the table for our three children and try and keep the lifestyle we were accustomed to, after five years of a depth of pain about the injustice thrust upon our beautiful family, winning a lawsuit that proved Larry's death was due to medical negligence absolutely did not make me happy. I did not feel joy or redemption;

what I felt was anger. I felt angry, and I felt bitter that on the day that should have been spent celebrating twenty-five years of marriage to each other, I was sharing the same space in a courtroom with the man whose mistake would prevent me from ever celebrating anything with my Larry again.

It would be years before I touched one cent of that money, and I never told a single person what we had "won." The fact that Larry was being represented by a price tag put a bad taste in my mouth; no amount of money was worth his life. I was used to working and supporting us, so I continued; even though Scott and I were married, I didn't expect him to be financially responsible for my children.

Over the years, I have heard many stories of medical negligence. Just because it can't be proven doesn't mean it did not happen. Scott could not prove that Sally was neglected, and he did not win his lawsuit, but I have no doubt that malpractice occurred.

At work the following day, a coworker of mine and I were talking, and I mentioned to her that Larry and I would have just been celebrating our twenty-fifth wedding anniversary. She proceeded to wish me a happy anniversary, and I was so taken aback by her saying those words that I literally said nothing in response and walked away. I couldn't stop obsessing about it all night, and when I saw her the next day, I approached her.

"I was venting to you," I said to my coworker Melissa. "The anniversary of what should have been twenty-five years is no longer a happy day for me. To say, "Happy Anniversary," to me is not appropriate."

She looked at me, defeated, and I could tell she felt sorry. "After I said that to you, I knew it was the wrong choice of words," she said.

"It's okay," I replied. "I just wanted to be honest. It was only happy when Larry was here to share it with me."

I see this in my groups all the time, on Facebook, on Instagram, and in our meetings. Some people want to be wished a happy anniversary, but for me, it changed once Larry was not here to share in the joy of what that day represented for both of us.

After that experience with Melissa, I thought more deeply about how we communicate our grief to others. People don't know what to say, and if we don't tell them, how can we expect them to learn? We can share our grief in a way that teaches people and doesn't offend them.

I now refer to our anniversary as "my love day with Larry," and I ask that people don't wish me a happy one. I learned what works for me, and I make sure the people in my life know how I feel. There is no wrong or right; it's what works for you.

I stayed with my grandmother for a full week after the trial. I was struggling with lying next to Scott in bed, feeling uncomfortable after being thrown back into the tragic space I shared with Larry on that dreadful day. I missed him, and I needed to escape. Scott completely understood.

My paternal grandmother lived to be ninety-six years old. Throughout the years, I have been told countless times that of all the "grandchildren" in our family, I am most like her. I started thinking about what my life would be like if I followed in her footsteps, and I realized that if I never remarried and lived to be as old as she was, I would be alone for fifty-four years.

Fifty-four years was a lot longer than the twenty-three that I spent with Larry when he was alive. I needed to remember these things; I needed to count my blessings and be grateful that I had anything to count at all.

I didn't even fold my clothes back into my suitcase. I threw them in there and flew back home to Scott.

CHAPTER 14

What Happened to Our Happily Ever After?

Things with Brett were getting worse. The substance abuse and the range of substances increased, and what started with marijuana and pills turned into cocaine and heroin. Scott and I struggled with how to handle everything, and we, for the first time, started to argue. We had no clue where to begin.

Desperate for help, I decided to go to our local gas station and show Brett's photo to the attendant who worked there. I asked him if he had ever seen Brett before, and when he confirmed he had, I pleaded with him never to sell beer or cigarettes to my underage son again. I didn't like the confused look on his face, so I raised my voice—just a little so that I knew he could clearly hear me—and I said, "If you sell my son beer again, it won't be just me who comes back. I'll bring the police!"

Brett later told me that the attendant would panic any time Brett went to that gas station after my exchange with him there.

I guess the guy got the message; unfortunately, however, Brett did not.

Our marriage was under stress, and Scott and I disagreed about how to deal with the stealing, the lying, the denying, and the disappearing. I felt like I couldn't leave the house because things that would be there one day would be missing the next.

We decided to send Brett to a rehabilitation clinic that effectively cost what would have been his college education. This upset us, but it was our only choice, and we had to do what we felt was in his best interest. We were able to visit him every weekend, and he was doing well, but as soon as he got out, he was back to using. There were constant visits from the police due to the arguments echoing off the walls of our home from the worry and grief. I was ashamed and desperate for help.

After therapists continued to affirm the obvious—that Brett was using drugs to escape from the pain of losing his mother—we put him in a children's mental hospital for a few weeks. All the while, I was still working full-time, facilitating widow's groups every Wednesday night, and trying to be there for our other five children.

When Brett got out, we gave him an ultimatum: "Clean up or get out." We were worried about our other children, and we had to hold him accountable for his behavior; enabling him by inviting him back home without consequence would not have helped, and we were out of options. Brett moved out the following year.

The Heartache of a Child's Addiction

A child who is suffering from drug abuse is the cause of ruin for many marriages. Scott and I had only been married for a few months when this was discovered, and our other children needed us. I was increasingly worried about what this was going to do to our relationship with each other and with all our children.

He may not have been living with us, but we were not going to desert him, so we hired a private detective to follow Brett and give us details about what he was doing and whom he was doing it with. He had hit rock bottom and was sharing his car with a teenage girl who had become his drug partner, and her mother, Brenda, was frequently driving by and keeping me updated on Brett.

Brenda had two of her own children who were also struggling with drugs, and she told me that a man had come to her house, put a gun to her head, and threatened to kill her if she didn't hand over the money her children had owed him.

She was real street; she told him to kill her because she had no money to give him.

What scared me the most was what could happen to Zach and Jordana if anyone were to come to our home because of Brett's actions. He was extremely close with his siblings, and if anyone wanted to get back at him for something, I feared his siblings would be the number one target. I made sure to watch the kids get on the bus each morning, and I was adamant that the nanny watch them get off the bus from school every afternoon. Brett decided to move to Albany for a girl he claimed he had fallen in love with. After a year, she broke it off with him, and he called us, begging us to come home.

After agreeing that he no longer had rights to his old room (we had given it to Zachary) and promising to undergo random drug tests, Brett moved back in. We were so excited the night that he returned. I made the family's favorite: macaroni and meatballs, set the table for a party, and lit up the fireplace. I was determined to make our house feel warm and welcoming, and I wanted Brett to feel what he had been missing. I wanted him to want us to be a whole family again. That evening went off without a hitch; he even helped me with the dishes. I could feel his gratitude and love for my forgiveness and believing in him to stay sober.

Things were looking up. Brett went back to college, maintained a 4.0 GPA at Suffolk Community College, and got accepted at Binghamton University, where he would be admitted as a physics major. The pride we felt in him was insurmountable—all those years of hell with drugs, and we were finally seeing the light.

During Brett's second year at school, Scott came to me one day and told me that Brett was looking into seeing a psychiatrist; he had it in his mind that he needed to use Adderall for help with his attention deficit disorder. I immediately became concerned and pleaded with Scott to call the psychiatrist to be sure he knew about Brett's history with drugs. Due to the HIPPA laws, the psychiatrist hung up on Scott before he was even able to voice his concerns.

Brett started to have hallucinations. We begged him to stop taking Adderall, but even off of them, the hallucinations continued. Now, we didn't know what to think, and we were questioning his mental health. The hallucinations were affecting his ability to study, and though he managed to graduate in May of that year, he barely passed any of his classes. I'll never forget being able to point him out in a crowd of over six hundred graduates on the day he graduated from Binghamton. I could hardly contain myself and screamed, "There he is!" rather loudly during what was supposed to be a quiet part of the ceremony. I didn't care. I was so proud of Brett on that day.

When he came home, he was very withdrawn, and while we were trying desperately to have things feel "normal" at home, Scott's dad took a turn for the worst; with his mother already suffering from severe Alzheimer's, Scott had to fly to Florida to be with both. While he was there, his dad passed away, and so did Sally's favorite uncle, Uncle Bernie, who was like a surrogate grandpa to my kids. While Scott and his sisters now had the added challenge of finding a nursing home for his mother, I was attending church daily, praying for my husband, and praying for our son, who was now slurring his words and looking paler and thinner by the day.

Scott and I were equally worried, so we visited Brett's psychologist on our own, on Brett's behalf. I explained everything I was observing at home, and we all agreed that it would be a good idea if I started to administer Brett's medication for him as he was acting more confused lately, and the last thing we wanted was for him to unintentionally take more than he required or could handle. I left feeling hopeful, but . . .

◇◇◇

One week later, August 14th, 2013, Brett was scheduled for therapy at seven o'clock in the evening.

I had been out running errands all day, so I had not been home for most of the morning, and though I usually check on him throughout the day, when I asked Anthony around one o'clock in the afternoon if he had seen Brett, he replied that he hadn't. I figured he was still sleeping from all of the medication he was on, and I went back out.

When dinner time arrived, and Brett had yet to come down from his room, I decided to go up and check on him myself. It just so happened that Jordana and her boyfriend at the time had come home, and she wanted to use the hot tub, so we both went upstairs together—I was to get Brett, and she wanted to get her bathing suit.

I called out his name repeatedly, but he never answered. I open his door, and I was finally able to breathe again when I saw him sleeping in his bed. "Brett, let's go. You have therapy in an hour!" I yelled with the hopes of waking him.

He didn't move.

I was horrified, and I immediately knew what had happened.

Scott was not yet home from work. I called Ella, immediately brought back to that fateful night when I found my Larry on our bedroom floor. I screamed what I think was "Brett is dead!" repeatedly into the phone, but later Ella told me that

I kept repeating "Larry is dead," and though she knew that could not be possible, she knew something terrible had happened and rushed over to be with me within minutes of hanging up the phone.

Our closest friends and family all came over. I felt like I was reliving the nightmare of Larry's death all over again.

I know now that Brett died from grief; the pain he was in from losing his biological mom caused him to take drugs, and the drugs caused his already broken heart to fail.

We gave him a Jewish funeral, just as Sally would have wanted, and Danielle and Zach wrote and delivered beautiful eulogies about their brother.

Bernie, Sally's favorite uncle, had died a few months before. His beautiful wife gave up her plot in the graveyard so that Brett could be buried beside his mom, so now, when I go to the cemetery, I visit them all.

I officially felt dead inside; even at church, where I was comforted and held by the community of people whom I have known throughout the years, I felt empty; I felt alone in my grief; I felt angry.

I found an empty chapel to go to, and I remember falling to my knees in front of the huge, ornate crucifix of Christ. I begged him to have mercy on Brett's soul, and through sobs and heavy breathing, spoke out loud to our Lord to help us all get through yet another loss.

"How is this possible," I screamed. "How can this happen to us? We have already suffered so much! I have been a dedicated follower. I followed the commandments daily. How,

Lord? Why?" I felt I had already carried my cross. This was just too heavy. It hurt not just for me but for Scott and my children.

When I couldn't cry anymore, I picked myself up and walked out of the chapel. One of my favorite nuns, Sister Kay, who helps me with bereavement, was standing outside the door, holding a piece of paper with scripture written on it, to give to me. She hugged me tightly and whispered, "Stay close to Scott." She knew the challenges that couples face when losing a child, but I knew our love for each other was too strong to break us.

Sister Kay, director of our groups at
St. Matthew's, Dix Hills, NY

New Waves of Grief

Scott went back to work right away, which contributed to my feeling that I was doing this alone. He did the same thing when Sally died, and he explained that this is what he needed to do to cope. He also made the decision not to tell anyone at work about what had happened to Brett. He did not want to be faced with the condolences, the questions, or the looks that both of us were all too familiar with from having lost our spouses.

I, on the other hand, could not even think about working; I was a total mess, and just getting dressed was difficult. Ella started coming over every day to encourage me to get up, and with her help, we managed to clean and repaint Brett's room. I didn't want to wait because I knew it would bring me back to my pain like it had with Larry. Scott immediately agreed to us doing this; we needed to paint over the reminder of what we'd lost between those walls. It didn't work, though; our other children

Brett at 23

avoided coming home because of the trauma we all experienced from that day, and we needed our children more than ever. We decided that we had to move.

I was going to an endocrinologist at the time who put me on a strict diet. Being on a controlled diet helped with my grief.

This was something I hadn't known. The fact that I had to think out, pre-plan, and write down everything gave me a little sense of control where I felt like I had none.

Sonia

I was in so much pain that I went to speak to one of the priests at my church. He encouraged me to take the focus off myself, and this made me feel ashamed. I started focusing more on swallowing my pride and deflating my ego to follow his advice.

One night, while watching the local news, a story popped up about a woman named Sonia. My attention was aroused when I heard that she, too was a widow, and then my heart sank into my chest when I saw her picture. After swerving from a motorcycle while driving on the expressway, Sonia crashed her car, and as a result, she was paralyzed from the neck down.

I was deeply affected by Sonia's story, and I was struggling with the amount of suffering people experience in our world. I wished there was something more I could do.

It just so happened that my older sister had to be admitted to the local hospital. I went to visit her, trying to keep myself busy because of the pain of my grief. When I arrived at her room, she was speaking with a chaplain and another man named Tom, who called himself a prayer warrior. She was telling them about my bereavement ministry, and Tom was interested in learning more, so we got to talking for quite a while. He was of Protestant faith, and he regularly visited prisons and hospitals to pray for people. I immediately thought of Sonia, and I explained her story, or at least what I had learned from the news. We agreed that she could use prayer, so he and I decided to visit her together at Stonybrook Hospital on the following day. I was taking the focus on myself, just like the priest I went to had advised me.

◇◇◇

Tom arrived at my home around ten in the morning, and we talked at length during the thirty-minute drive to the hospital. I told him about Brett, and I told him about Larry, and I told him how I needed to take my focus off my own pain. He listened to me with sincere compassion. We forged a friendship that day on our way to pray for someone else.

Before we got out of the car to go into the hospital, Tom asked me if I knew what Sonia's faith was, and it occurred to me that I didn't, but for some reason, I had a feeling that, like me, she was Catholic and she was. He acknowledged that it did not matter, and we proceeded together toward the front doors of the ICU.

She was intubated and unable to speak, but I was told that she could hear me. "I heard your story on the news," I said, "and I am also a widow. I have been feeling a need to pray for you." I introduced Tom, who was standing beside me, and I asked her if it was okay for us to pray.

Tears were streaming down both of our faces, and she nodded as if to say, "Yes." Tom started anointing Sonia with oil and by referring to God as "Father God."

He continues to ask, "Father God, let your fire heal her," and when he was done, I recited The Lord's Prayer and a Hail Mary. I took her hand, and while locking eyes, I promised her that every day, at three o'clock, I would pray for her. I knew three o-clock was the time of day Christ had died, and I was typically in the chapel at that time.

Tom's prayer style was a little overly dramatic from what I was accustomed to, but I could still appreciate it. When we were walking to the elevator, he asked for my opinion, and I was honest with him. I told him the fire part was a bit too heavy for me, and that fire made me think immediately of Hell. Confused, he looked at me and asked, "Did God not show up in the burning bush?" He continued, "Did not the apostles have tongues of fire over them?" He was right, and I was wrong, and I was impressed.

At that very moment, a young Hasidic man entered the elevator, and all I could think was, "A Jew, a Catholic, and a Protestant walked into an elevator . . . ," and without being able to control myself, I started to giggle. I whispered the joke to Tom, and he started to laugh. I realize it was the first time I'd really laughed since Brett died.

When I got home, I was determined to pull myself together and continue with my bereavement groups for widows and widowers. Taking the focus off myself was exactly what I needed, and even that short period of time with Tom and Sonia made all the difference, but the challenges that would come from coping with Brett's death would prove to be very difficult.

◇◇◇

"Now we can't call you guys the Brady Bunch!" Two weeks after Brett's passing, a friend of ours ignorantly made this comment, and I literally felt as though I had been punched in the stomach. I had already learned from losing Larry that people simply say and do things without thinking; they don't wish to hurt me intentionally, so I said nothing in response and walked away.

Our first Christmas without Brett was particularly hard. Scott wanted everything to be the same, and I simply did not have it in me to keep up the façade. I needed to buy new ornaments because the ones we had were decorated with each of our children's names, and it was simply too hard to go through each of them. It was during Christmas dinner, however, that I snapped. My PTSD was affecting every aspect of my ability to function, and when I could not keep track of what I was even cooking, I had a meltdown.

Scott later apologized for pushing me too hard. He was determined to hold onto some form of "normal," while I completely lost track of what "normal" even was. Somehow, we managed to find a new normal together.

Many of my widows and widowers supported us by coming to the funeral parlor and to our home. In a guest book at the funeral home (for family and friends to sign so you can thank them properly), one man wrote "NO THANK YOU NECESSARY, RONNIE" in all capital letters and with nothing else. Writing thank-you cards while grieving is an absolute nightmare, and ever since Ronnie wrote this in our book, I have written it in every one I have signed since Brett's passing. I always share this with my groups; sometimes, there are little things we can do to prevent a whole lot of pain.

CHAPTER 15

On Our Knees,
We Are All Equal

I learned that empathy lasts longer than sympathy. It takes the focus off *you*.

My trauma from my losses was causing me to have difficulties with simple things, and I needed help if I wanted to move forward with my groups in September. I called my assistant, Arlene, and I explained my concerns. We agreed that I would run the groups based on my memory, and if I were to forget anything, she would read along and fill in the holes as needed.

We had twenty-three members in this group, and for the first time, I realized that giving back to others was helping me to heal. For seven years, it was just Arlene and me, and we couldn't get anyone to help us. But after this group, I shared how giving back to them helped me heal. Two members eagerly trained to become facilitators for my teen group.

Learning that giving back helps with healing was a concept up until this point, I had not learned.

Arlene and me

When I started my bereavement groups, my only intention was to give widows more support than what was available to me when I first lost my husband. What started with one group and one facilitator now, after learning about another way to heal, turned into twelve groups presently and thirty facilitators, not counting those who went off on their own—all volunteers, all trained, some of whom have stayed with us for over five years. I am so grateful to every volunteer who has helped me help others. They have truly given me and others the greatest gift: their time.

A few months after starting up again, I wrote to the priest who had given me the advice to take the focus off myself. In a card, I thanked him for helping me, and it was at that moment that I realized just as a priest had saved my mother's life all those years ago, a priest was now saving mine.

I was continuing to facilitate groups, but I was struggling. Without being able to focus long enough to even read a book, I felt like I was all over the place; I couldn't believe I was living through this again.

Eventually, I forced myself to listen to audiobooks on self-help, and that was what I needed to start pushing through. I wrote notes while listening, and I found YouTube videos with daily motivational messages delivered by speakers who are experts in their field. This was so helpful in my healing; most of this was not available when I lost Larry.

When it comes to the way we choose to live our lives after the one we planned on living is ripped away from us, we need to be more understanding of how others choose to live theirs. We simply do not know what lies ahead, and if we let people determine our own timeline for us, we will become prisoners to their judgment and skeptics of our own.

I asked my group once, "What would you wish for your spouse if it happened the other way around." and everyone's comments were similar. They wrote that they would wish them to live life to the fullest and enjoy whatever time they had left.

As I continue to open my perspective and awareness of what suffering means, my compassion grows for others, and the limits imposed upon me by my own pain continue to decrease.

An old Italian saying suggests that if you were asked to write down your troubles on a piece of paper, put it in the middle of a table with papers that are detailed with other people's troubles; upon reading what others were struggling with, you would choose to keep your own. After listening to so many horrific stories throughout the years, I can claim this to be true.

We must help ourselves through grief; no one is going to knock on our doors and save us. We must save ourselves. If we do nothing to help ourselves in five years, we will be exactly where we are now, five years down the line. I have witnessed it happen, and it often ends with regret, if it ends at all.

I've said it before, and I will say it again: If you do not change something, nothing will.

We are All Entitled to Our Beliefs

I am not proselytizing; I am just sharing what I believe. I feel I am incredibly enriched by my relationship with my faith, but I feel strongly about distancing religion from my groups. I don't want to cause anyone to feel as though I am pushing my religion on them, and I want widows and widowers of every faith to feel encouraged to join.

I am always clear about how I feel, and I hold no judgment toward my members for their beliefs, sexual preferences, political attachments, etc. I am not here to judge beliefs; I'm here to guide people through their grief. And while God teaches me to love everyone the way I love myself, it's important to leave judgment out. I have many who are exactly how I was: lukewarm in their faith or no faith at all.

Contending with grief is a challenge we can almost count on in life—some more prematurely than others—and throughout my relationship with it, I have learned these words to be most true: to make a difference in someone's life, you don't have to be brilliant, rich, beautiful, or perfect; you just have to care.

The COVID pandemic forced many of us to reflect what it means to be alone, and the truth is that life is so much better surrounded by people we love. Connections help us grow, and without them, loneliness can be all-consuming.

The year 2020 was one of the worst years for grief and loss, not only because so many lost loved ones to the virus but also because of the limited ability to connect with family and friends for support in the aftermath. The heavy burden of being alone that came with the lockdown has lifted; however, those who know loss as we do are burdened more deeply with the task of learning to live in a place that many of us now define as "a new normal."

During that year, I trained two women—one from Ghana and one from Malaysia—to facilitate bereavement groups in their countries, both of which had little to no resources for those struggling with grief. I also helped women from Ireland, Columbia, and Australia. It felt purposeful to be able to help widows from other countries. I truly take this work seriously.

In Amy Morin's book, *13 Things Mentally Strong People Do Not Do*, she explains that taking the focus off the things we cannot control, and focusing only on what we can, will enable us to accomplish so much more than we ever imagined we could. I received this same advice from my priest after losing Brett, and as I continue to read more, learn more, and meet more people, I'm discovering the true value in its message. My hope is that

I'm able to impart the gravity of this message to everyone in my life who needs to hear it and that, with time, they begin to believe in it, just as I have.

I often wondered, after Larry passed, if God was punishing me. I was not perfect, and I started to reflect my past: who I was, and what I must have done to deserve this pain. Sometimes, Larry and I would argue over ridiculous things. We didn't expect this to happen. Was God angry with me for taking Larry for granted?

I knew these were just intrusive thoughts—not facts—but they were constantly invading my mind. Many widows say the same thing to me: "Am I being punished?" I am not qualified to know the answers to that. God instructs us in the Bible to take care of the widow, the orphan, and the foreigner. Sounds like God cares about the widow to me.

After the loss, so many of us may suffer from regret, or we may find ourselves pointing our fingers and pointing out blame to others and to ourselves.

When I made the choice to dedicate much of my life to those who are grieving, I made the choice to be surrounded by death, and perhaps the biggest shock of all is the incredible number of people who have suffered such intense, crippling pains of grief. My biggest surprise is I had no idea how many young widows and widowers there were.

People often struggle with questions of their own mortality; it's hard to come to terms with the inevitability of death. Some people even believe that planning a will can cause their demise sooner, and they struggle to recognize the difference between facts and their thoughts. Facts need evidence to support them, and there is no evidence to support this.

Working with widows and widowers in bereavement groups has never been a job for me; instead, it has become my life's purpose, and it is because of my continued efforts with grief and assisting others with theirs that I have met the most incredible people.

Three years ago, I decided to stop running my own groups. Now, many of my past members have gone through extensive training to facilitate, which enables me to oversee everything, engage with all my members, and work independently with those who are struggling.

I once paid a small fortune for a course in life coaching. The instructor of this course felt very strongly about the monetary value associated with counseling, and she was adamant in her belief that "the money you charge your clients is indicative of the value you think you are worth."

Many of my members are unemployed or are struggling under the added stress of losing a second income. Charging people an exorbitant amount of money to help them with their grief never quite sat well with me, especially since I believe compassion doesn't have a price.

Larry and I had a plan, we shared an extraordinary love, and we built an incredible life together. When I lost him, I was tortured by the derailment of our plan, and my world turned into one with which I struggled to survive. All the platitudes that were pushed upon me during the early months of my loss felt insulting, but hindsight has shown me and enabled me to appreciate the growth I have attained in business, my personal life, and spirituality, which would have never come to fruition if not for my loss.

My lack of schooling has sometimes caused me to feel self-conscious in certain situations; however, when helping those with grief, I feel less intimidated by the many very educated members because of all I have learned about grief over the years. The experience of grief that we share brings us all to our knees, and on our knees, we are all equal.

The obstacles that I have endured, though painful, have provided me with the platform to help others. I once heard that if we are looking in the rear-view mirror while driving forward, then we will most definitely crash. We can't keep looking back into our past as we are trying to go forward; I carry my loss beside me as I walk forward in this life. I learned how to move it from being in front of me, and after a while, I stopped tripping over it.

CHAPTER 16

A New and Different Grief

Stephen Colbert once asked Keanu Reeves what he thinks happens to us when we die." I felt his response to be so touching that I immediately shared it on my Instagram: "I know that the ones who love us will miss us."

When you have been touched by loss, you can recognize those who have been touched by it, too.

It starts at such a young age: the first time we separated from our parents, we felt the loss.

The first class we left, the favorite teacher we left behind, the first friend who moved away, the pets we lost.

The childhood we outgrew.

As we mature, we lose the homes we once lived in and the friends we made there. Those of us who have children lose the freedom of the life we had before them.

When our first child leaves home, we grieve for them. When they all move out and our once-lively homes become empty nests, we grieve again, and as our parents age, we grieve the loss of their youth, knowing that we too will lose our own.

In some cases, we even grieve the end of a career that we may have loved or may not have loved but that somehow managed to, in some capacity, define us.

But there is no grief greater than that which grows from death, from losing someone we love. Some losses might be expected and some might not, but what emerges from the loss is a complete shift from the lives we once knew, so blindsided by the pain that we even lose all recognition of ourselves.

After enduring loss throughout our lives, you would think we would develop some kind of resilience but the bitter truth is that, for this, we have nothing.

I had to learn to accept new beginnings and cherish memories. Yet even now as I write this, I know tomorrow's changes may change my thoughts about today. We often expect things to be different than they become, but many times the choices are not ours to make.

On April of 2023, the handsome John Diaz of CBS News asked me to participate in a segment on *Community Heroes*. At that time, I had fifteen widows who desperately needed a group and no one available to facilitate them. Having no other choice, I stepped back into my old facilitating role with the same ease it takes to get back on a bike, picking up right where I had left off nearly three years prior. I always loved running my own group. Always looking for ways to expose our groups to those in need, I knew this was a great opportunity, so I agreed to allow it.

What he came to see was the reality of how a real group operates, and on Sunday, May 6th, at nine o'clock in the morning, the segment aired for his viewers to see, as well.

As luck would have it, I was vacationing in California that morning, unable to tune in from the hotel, but I knew it had been released by the many calls I simultaneously received. Of those calls, the most unusual came from my breast doctor, excited to have seen me and taken aback by learning of the work I was committed to. After many congratulations, she explained that upon reviewing my chart for my phone number, she realized that I was due for a mammogram and ultrasound. Though I didn't keep track of every time I went for a screening over the past twenty years, I knew for certain that I never missed a screening, except for the year of the pandemic and the year after. In 2004, I underwent a lumpectomy on my right breast, and consequently took medication for a few years, which was when my relationship with this particular doctor had begun. Heeding her call, I immediately made an appointment a days following my return from the West Coast.

The Word No One Wants to Hear

Shortly thereafter, on July 26th, I officially became a cancer patient, diagnosed with Stage 2 triple negative inductal breast cancer. An aggressive, 2.5-centimeter tumor had grown in my left breast very close to my chest muscle, a condition affecting only 15 percent of women studied. This particular strain is more prominent in African-American women and women under the age of fifty, yet somehow, I had it too.

I didn't smoke. I didn't drink. I exercised daily, and my weight was perfect for my height. How the hell could I have breast cancer?

I was looking at five months of chemo, followed by surgery and radiation. I would lose all my hair, and, oddly, I had to remove my acrylic nails (apparently, the UV rays from the nail salons is carcinogenic). I couldn't eat salads or any raw food, and everything I even considered putting into my mouth had to be washed thoroughly. I was so susceptible to bacteria that I couldn't eat a banana without first washing its peel!

My isolation from others was unquestionable. After years of hearing many stories about people who had died not from the cancer they were battling, but from contracting a cold, the flu, COVID, pneumonia, sepsis, or something else passed on from an unsuspecting bystander, not only was my facilitating role put on hold, but I was robbed of the joy and warmth I received when sharing space with my family and beautiful grandchildren. Cancer took away my sunshine.

I started chemo in the second week of August, overcome with thoughts of horror stories from widowers who had lost their wives to only one chemo treatment.

◇◇◇

After being forewarned by another patient of cancer that losing my hair would not only be traumatic but also painful, I cut my hair into a bob in preparation. It hurt anyway. My scalp was so sensitive that I could hardly lay on a pillow, and after only two weeks, I shed like a dog. Large amounts of hair would turn up all around the house, and it was clear that I had no choice but to call my hairdresser to shave my head. The little hair that remained slid right off into my hands as I washed my head the very first time, and I was completely bald. The trauma of that moment is simply hard to explain.

This grief was new and so incredibly heavy. I felt like I had lost my womanhood, my femininity. I lost everything about myself, and I couldn't even look in the mirror to try and find where that lost woman was. I can vividly remember eating dinner with Scott during one particularly hot night. I became so overheated that I had to pull the seemingly permanent knit cap from off of my head to get some relief. Scott looked over at me and quickly looked away. In that moment, I felt more exposed, vulnerable, and ugly than I had ever felt in my entire life.

Grief Again

For two weeks, crying accompanied every breath I took. I wept while trying to eat breakfast, and I wept while taking a shower. The reflection that appeared in the glass shower door was of a stranger, and upon seeing her, I sobbed and sobbed. I was quickly thrown back into the depths of grief I felt when I lost Larry, and though Scott would gently ask me not to cry, I knew I needed to; I needed to get it out or I would make myself sicker than I already was. I needed to grieve my hair; I needed to grieve my nails; I needed to grieve the uncertainty I was facing about my life all over again.

After two weeks of uncontrollable crying, I found a therapist, and it was then that thoughts of one of our members, Laurie, prevailed.

Laurie was a young widow who had been diagnosed with
vulva cancer and sadly died before I received my diagnosis. I
watched her lose so much before she lost her life, leaving behind
her thirteen-year-old daughter and seventeen-year-old autistic
son who had lost their father only three years before. When I
closed my eyes, the image of her in a coffin permeated my sight,
and my thoughts started to turn very dark. I felt if God could
take her, he could certainly take me, too, and I was overcome
with worry for my children. I couldn't imagine them having to
go through another loss after all we had been through, and I
worried for Scott, who had already lost so much with Sally and
Brett. He was good at hiding it, sure, but I knew how worried
he really was.

Everyone kept telling me to stay positive. Zachary pushed
me to get my paints out and to not spend all my time thinking about cancer. He was right; I needed something to occupy
my mind, but it was so difficult. I managed to find solace in
painting cards for the nurses who cared for me during my
chemo treatment each week. Into each of them, I would place
a Starbucks gift card, thanking them for their service and
kindness. They were all so compassionate and kind, and in
the end, they shared with me that every card received was
displayed in their lockers.

I continued to walk each day, with only some exceptions.
There were times that the treatment knocked me out, and all I

Staying positive

could do was lay on the couch. On many nights, I couldn't sleep; the steroids caused me to wake up after dozing off for about an hour, and I'd be up for the rest of the night. In an attempt to not disturb Scott, I'd leave the bedroom for the downstairs den. The rest of the day was spent sleeping on and off. This soon became a weekly challenge.

Three months after my diagnosis, Ella's husband was diagnosed with Stage 4 throat cancer. He needed her support, too, and although she still managed to bring me meals and talk with me daily, for the first time in all the time we had known each other, we couldn't be there for each other like we wanted to, like we needed to.

When October arrived, I was feeling defeated. Looking at the calendar, marked with weeks upon weeks of treatments that still remained, was causing me to feel so overwhelmed that the thought of undergoing all of them seemed impossible.

With nowhere else to turn, I called my church and went to see a priest. We spoke at length, and I was grateful for his support, but it was when he asked me about finding the cancer that he enlightened me. I told him I hadn't known I had cancer and explained the story of my doctor having seen me on the news.

"That's divine intervention," he said. "You are going to be okay."

He blessed me, gave me communion, and assured me that in time, I would understand why I was going through this. My treatment on the very next day was postponed—my red blood cell count was too low, and I needed a blood transfusion.

I journaled, walked, went to therapy, painted, and prayed to get myself through the remaining treatments. In order to determine whether or not the chemo had worked, I had to undergo an MRI. Oncologists define a response to treatment as a decrease in tumor mass of at least 50 percent; mine was 80 percent, and only 20 percent of the tumor remained.

On January 23, 2024, I had surgery to remove the remainder of the tumor, and on January 31st, it was determined that I was cancer free. I believe in the power of prayer and its role in my healing. Six weeks later, I started a three-week cycle of radiation, and now, six months later as I'm writing this, I'm back on my feet and receiving compliments on my cute pixie haircut.

I'll never forget the feeling of embracing my family again for the first time after being cleared, and I'll never be without the pain of knowing that Laurie never got the chance to embrace hers. I know the prayers for Laurie worked in their own way, but it's hard to fathom why a young woman with so many reasons to be here lost her life while I kept mine. There is not a day that goes by that I don't think about her, and I will forever keep her family in my prayers.

◇◇◇

I wanted to include this chapter at the end of my book because cancer revealed to me a completely different side of grief that I otherwise would never have understood. Returning to social situations and encountering people who didn't immediately recognize me with my short hair and steroid-induced weight gain caused me to feel uncomfortable in such a way that I felt the need to provide an explanation for my appearance. I still didn't feel like myself—a common feeling associated with grief when it strikes its ugly face. I recognized it for what it was, and I learned how to use my coping skills as a young widow to help me adapt to a life post cancer.

When I lost Larry, I lost my world, yet I always remained grateful for the life we were so blessed to have had together. Similarly, undergoing cancer treatment and having survived it has changed my world yet again; this time, however, I remain grateful just to be alive. Miraculously Ella's husband also survived his cancer.

Please go for your mammogram; it saves lives.

AFTERWORD

My beautiful, blended family with Scott has grown.
Zachary went to medical school and became a doctor. Jordana is an attorney and is engaged to a wonderful man. Scott and I are incredibly proud of their accomplishments.

Both Michael and Anthony are married with children of their own. They had large shoes to fill but filled them entirely—just like their father. Like my Larry, their love is fierce, and their commitment to their family is strong. Also, like Larry, they are both businessmen. They live two minutes from each other and are raising their children together. I love the women they chose as their wives, two more daughters to love like my own.

Danielle is married to a wonderful man and gave birth to their first baby. I'm proud to say she grew into the lady Larry always wanted her to be. He would be so incredibly proud of all our children.

Like many, Scott and I are proud of our kids, but I think those of us who had to do this solo feel it was a more difficult path for them to cope with loss and all the changes life threw at us unexpectedly. I am glad that I can tell others my story with the hopes of knowing we can get through this. My son

Anthony said to me one day, "Mom, I 'm proud of you and all you did, and the many things you do for others." What could be better than that? I also recognize that I, too, have a legacy to leave behind.

I do not have all the answers, and much of life will always be somewhat of a mystery, but learning more about my faith has helped me to understand some of the whys that many of us who have experienced loss find most difficult to understand.

It provides grounding for me like an anchor. I know whatever time I have left on Earth is here for God; he created me for him. I didn't ask to be here, and I am grateful for the journey of time I was given. My Larry and Brett both taught me how short life really is because they died; I lived it in a way I never thought possible.

"In a hundred years, we will all be dead."

The words my sister spoke to me at Larry's wake will forever inspire me—not the day I was born, nor the day I will die, but all the days that are in between and what I choose to do with each of them.

◇◇◇

My loss and all it encompasses has changed the trajectory of my life and inspired me to read the Bible.

I noticed early on that those in my group who had faith, whatever it was, seemed to be handling their grief better than I did, and this made me curious. I must thank my groups for sharing their beliefs; we never know what life has in store for us, as you very well know. In the blink of an eye, our whole world can be flipped around.

If not for my loss, I would have never picked up the Bible. You could have hit me over the head with a pan, and still, you would not have garnered my attention. In losing Larry, I sought more, and from seeking more, I grew spiritually.

I believe Larry's death, in some way, saved my soul. I have what they call magical thinking, so I sometimes envision different things in my mind; I had this vision of God asking Larry if he wanted to save me and Larry saying, "I would give my life for her."

I imagine God then posed to Larry, "You could spend sixty years with Kathryn, and she will never come to me, or you can spend twenty years with her. If you die, you will save her soul because she will seek me, and you and Kathryn will have trillions of years in eternity together."

Larry's death has made me realize how important God is in my life. I believe his goal was coupled with my goal.

Take your gripes and make a difference with them; use the energy that emerges from your pain to help others and push your fears away. It says three hundred and sixty-five times in the Bible, "Do not be afraid." Trust that they are safe, and you will somehow be okay.

When I left behind the excuses, I learned how capable I truly was and how limiting my thoughts could be. Sister Anthony's belief in me from the very beginning became my calling, and it is the catalyst for the love, support, and guidance

I have been able to provide for every widow and widower with whom I have met over the past seventeen years.

My pain and suffering brought me to learn more about my faith. It is crazy that because of one person dying, I have helped thousands. That is significant. It did take me years to reflect and recognize this. There is so much personal growth in loss if we allow ourselves to learn. My therapist said to me one day, "What makes you think God didn't have a plan?"

Look at all you have done with your grief. I am far from perfect, but I know the grace of God is over me by the fruit my purpose has produced.

I listen to stories of loss every day—sometimes multiple times by all those who call looking for a group. I am reminded of just how precious this life is. We each have a cup to fill, and when it is full, our time on this earth will be complete. It does not have to do with who we marry or how many children we have, but rather what our soul is tasked with to complete in this lifetime. We each have a mission, but if we don't look for it, we'll never know what it is.

I'll admit to my near rejection of my own calling at first. Navigating Brett's addiction was so overwhelming that I felt myself giving up more than once; his passing almost pushed me over the edge, but my heart and soul guided me otherwise. I could not wait for my life to be perfect to help others. There is no such thing.

Someone said to me that God uses me as a vessel, and I like that because it gives him the glory. I would never believe I would be capable of doing all that I have done.

After five moves and being remarried for nineteen years, not a day goes by that I don't think about my Larry. He was taken from us twenty-three years ago, and my love for him still beats on.

THE DASH

By Linda Ellis

I read of a man who stood to speak
at the funeral of a friend.
He referred to the dates on the tombstone
from the beginning . . . to the end.

He noted that first came the date of birth
and spoke the following date with tears,
but he said what mattered most of all
was the dash between those years.

For that dash represents all the time
that they spent alive on earth.
And now only those who loved them
know what that little line is worth.

For it matters not, how much we own,
the cars . . . the house . . . the cash.
What matters is how we live and love
and how we spend our dash.

So, think about this long and hard.
Are there things you'd like to change?
For you never know how much time is left
that can still be rearranged.

If we could just slow down enough
to consider what's true and real
and always try to understand
?the way other people feel.

And be less quick to anger
and show appreciation more
and love the people in our lives
like we've never loved before.

If we treat each other with respect
and more often wear a smile,
remembering that this special dash
might only last a little while.

So, when your eulogy is being read,
with your life's actions to rehash . . .
would you be proud of the things they say
about how you spent YOUR dash?

RECOMMENDED BOOKS

Recommended books to help you during your grief journey:

Love and Compassion, by Kristen Neff
Honoring The Self, by Nathan Branden
The Body Keeps the Score, by Bessel Van Der Kolk, M.D.
The Grieving Brain, by Mary-Frances O'Connor, Ph.D.
The Grief Recovery Handbook, by John W. James and Russell
   Friedman
Every Memory Deserves Respect, by Michael Baldwin and Deb-
   orah L. Korn, Psy.D.
Who Moved My Cheese, by Spencer Johnson, M.D.
Out of the Maze, by Spencer Johnson, M.D.
Unwinding Anxiety, by Judson Brewer, M.D. , Ph.D.
A Grief Observed, by C.S. Lewis
13 Things Mentally Strong People Don't Do, by Amy Morin (see
   her TED talk)
The Well-Lived Life, by Gladys McGarey, M.D.

Books I didn't mention but that are helpful reading:

Option B, by Sheryl Sandberg and Adam Grant
Bearing the Unbearable, by Joanne Cacciatore, Ph.D.

The Four Agreements, by Don Miguel Ruiz
Sleep Smarter, by Shawn Stevenson
After, by Bruce Greyson, M.D.
Man's Search for Meaning, by Victor E. Frankl
The Joy of Well-Being, by Colleen and Jason Wachob
Creating a Life that Matters, by Manis Friedman and Rivka
   Goldstein (Judaism)

ACKNOWLEDGMENTS

First of all, I want to acknowledge my husband, Scott, because if it weren't for his support and understanding, I would not be able to do the work that I do. He has walked this journey with me in so many ways. Over the years, he has given up countless evenings of my company and hot dinners so I could be away leading support group meetings.

And then, my children, whom I also left weekly. They were so patient and understanding and giving of their mom, when they too, were grieving and processing, so that I could help other families who were going through what they were.

I want to thank my many grief group facilitators, starting with Arlene, all the way through to those who are still training. How grateful I am that you find this work as important as I do, to help other widows and widowers in their need and hardship. The ripple effects of your impact are quite amazing. Now we help hundreds of people each year instead of tens or twenties.

And then, Antonella, for her support and for reading and re-reading the manuscript with me.

Tysha, Violet, and Cheryl, who were my first beta readers and who gave me valuable "widow input," and Jean Duane, a fellow author who provided direction as I was writing.

My sisters and lifelong friends, Roseanne and Lisa, who were my support from the minute I lost Larry and Brett; I could not have done this—or life—without them.

My group members, for always being there for each other. I am so thankful for them all. We have grown together in many ways, in helping each other daily.

Alyson Lorenzo, a young widow herself, who spent countless hours going over the manuscript with me and offering wisdom and advice. She was my first editor.

And then Arlyn Lawrence, of Inspira Literary Solutions, who came in as the final editor, oversaw the design and book packaging, and brought it across the finish line for publication; I am grateful for her and her team.

Fun fact: Alyson's last name, "Lorenzo," is Italian for "Lawrence," which is Arlyn's last name, and of course was my first husband's, Larry's, given name. I believe this is no coincidence—or, as we say in our groups, a "God-incidence." I am one who likes to look for "signs" from God, and this was one of them. I truly have felt guided from above, from start to finish.

ABOUT THE AUTHOR

Kathryn Monaco Douglas was widowed at 42 and used this tragedy in her own life to help others work through their grief. Kathryn has been coaching and facilitating grief support groups for close to two decades. She has been featured multiple times on CBS News and News 12 as well as a guest on many podcasts relating to grief. Numerous articles have also been written about Kathryn and the work she is doing for young widows and widowers. Kathryn resides in Long Island, New York with her second husband, who was also widowed. For more information on Kathryn's groups, visit www.widowednotalone.com.

In Memory of Kim Gatto, who donated to have this book happen in order to help others from afar.

Donations to Widowednotalone to help widows with hardship can be made to:

Widowednotalone, Inc.
P.O. Box 223
Bay Shore, NY 11706

www.ingramcontent.com/pod-product-compliance
Lightning Source LLC
Jackson TN
JSHW021039231224
75924JS00001B/2